168

Bethune

BETHUNE

a
play
by
Rod
Langley

Vancouver, Talonbooks, 1975

Published with the assistance of the Canada Council

Talonbooks
201 - 1019 East Cordova
Vancouver, British Columbia
Canada V6A 1M8

This book was typeset by Linda Gilbert and printed in Canada by Hignell Printing Ltd.

Third Printing: July 1995

ACKNOWLEDGEMENTS: Roderick Stewart's *Bethune*, Gabriel Nadeau's *T.B.'s Progress*, The National Film Board of Canada, Terence Filgate of CBC's *Arts & Science*, Dr. John Routley and the contributions of the many people the author interviewed who knew Norman Bethune either personally or professionally.

In some productions, the full text of this play has been cut in the interest of brevity. For details, please write the author.

Canadian Cataloguing in Publication Data

Langley, Rod, 1942-
   Bethune

   ISBN 0-88922-088-3 pa.

   1. Bethune, Norman, 1890-1939 — Drama.
   I. Title.
PS8573.A53B4   C812'.5'4   C75-4393-8
PR9199.3.L35B4

for my mother,
Delis Marie Langley

Bethune was co-commissioned by the Saskatchewan Co-operative Credit Society and the Globe Theatre, Regina and Centaur Theatre, Montreal. It was first performed at the Globe Theatre, Regina, Saskatchewan, on November 5, 1974, with the following cast:

Dr. Norman Bethune	Kenneth Kramer
Frances Penney Bethune	Paddy Campanaro

In Detroit

Porter	Dana Still
Assistant Director	L'yn Ivall
Matron	Maureen Press
Miss Scarlet	Nicole Evans
Greely	Brian Tree
Nurse	Maureen Press
Friends of Bethune	L'yn Ivall, Nicole Evans

At Trudeau Sanitorium, New York State

McKenna	Dana Still
Nurse	Maureen Press

In Edinburgh

Mr. Penney	Stephen Walsh
Mrs. Penney	Maureen Press
Brigit	Nicole Evans

In Montreal

Dr. Edward Archibald	Michael Collins
Director	Dana Still
Accountant	L'yn Ivall
Matron	Maureen Press
Kon	Stephen Walsh
R.E. Coleman	Brian Tree

In Spain

Colonel	Michael Collins
Sorenson	Stephen Walsh
Orderly	Brian Tree
Soldiers	Dana Still, L'yn Ivall
Guard	L'yn Ivall
Prostitute	Nicole Evans
General Calabras	L'yn Ivall
Kon	Stephen Walsh

In China

Tung	Stephen Walsh
Ma Hall	Maureen Press
General Nieh	Brian Tree
Patients	Michael Collins, Dana Still
Bethune's Assistants	L'yn Ivall, Nicole Evans
Guard	Dana Still

Directed by Robert Sime

Bethune was also performed at the Centaur Theatre, Montreal, Quebec, on February 6, 1975, with the following cast:

Dr. Norman Bethune	Neil Vipond
Frances Penney Bethune	B.J. Gordon

In Detroit

Porter	Bob Aarron
Assistant Director	Martin Kevan
Matron	Ann Wickham
Miss Scarlet	Wenna Shaw
Greely	Roger Stevens
Friends of Bethune	Ann Wickham, Patrick Boxhill
Nurse	Wenna Shaw

At Trudeau Sanitorium, New York State

McKenna	Walter Massey
Nurse	Wenna Shaw

In Edinburgh

Mr. Penney	Walter Massey
Mrs. Penney	Ann Wickham
Brigit	Wenna Shaw

In Montreal

Dr. Archibald	Patrick Boxhill
Director	Bob Aarron
Accountant	John Peters
Matron	Joy Coghill
Kon	Walter Massey
R.E. Coleman	Roger Stevens

In Spain

Colonel	Bob Aarron
Sorenson	Martin Kevan
Prostitute	Wenna Shaw
General Calabras	Patrick Boxhill
Kon	Walter Massey
Members of the Press	Wenna Shaw, Ann Wickham
	Roger Stevens
Soldiers	Walter Massey, Chris Li,
	Michael Meagher, John Peters

In China

Tung	Chris Li
Ma Hall	Joy Coghill
General Nieh	Bob Aarron
Medical Assistant	Wenna Shaw
Soldiers	John Peters, Michael Meagher,
	Martin Kevan
Japanese Casualty	Walter Massey

Directed by George Plawski
Designed by Marti Wright
Lighting by Tim Williamson

ACT ONE

Scene 1

TUNG: My name is Tung.   *He bows.*
I wish to tell you of our Doctor.
Our Doctor, Bethune.
He came to us at the far end of the world.
It was a difficult journey for him.
He began at the centre of the world.

Railway station sounds are heard.

BETHUNE: Porter!   *Happily.*   Come on, Frances.
Don't dawdle.   *He grabs FRANCES' bags.*
Porter! Come on.

FRANCES: *staring around*   It's so . . . so dirty.

BETHUNE: We'll have none of your prissy colonialism
here, my girl. This is the new world. That black smoke is
merely the exhaust of industry — freedom — the centre
of the world. Porter! Detroit takes in hundreds of new
citizens everyday. Here, a man can make his fortune
overnight with astuteness and daring. I read how a
common workman went from rags to riches by just
designing a new bumper for Mr. Ford. It's a gold rush.
It's exciting. Here, I'll succeed — I promise you, Frances.

The honeymoon is over, thank God. It's hard work and accomplishment now — a new day.   *To Detroit.* Watch out, Norman B. is here!

FRANCES: Don't. Everybody thinks you're drunk.

BETHUNE: *louder*   I am drunk. You hear that, you beautiful bastards. I am drunk. Drunk on it all!

The PORTER takes his bags very sullenly and looks at BETHUNE as if he's mad. He takes the bags to stage right, plops them down and holds out his hand.

BETHUNE: Cheerful bastard.   *He holds up a $10.00 bill.*   Smile. That's right, you bastard. Broader!

FRANCES: *softly*   Oh my God.

BETHUNE: Broader. Hold it. That's right. Frances. Come on. Hold it . . .   *He threatens to take the $10.00 bill away.*   Frances.

He motions her to take a photograph of the PORTER.

FRANCES: Beth!

BETHUNE: Quick!

FRANCES takes a photograph.

BETHUNE: Thank you.

He gives the PORTER the $10.00 bill. FRANCES has her face buried in her hands. BETHUNE takes the PORTER's hat. When FRANCES looks up, she is staring at BETHUNE with the PORTER's cap on, with the same solemn expression. FRANCES tries not to laugh, but finally can't help it. They both laugh and BETHUNE picks her up and whirls her around.

FRANCES: That was cruel.

BETHUNE: So is free enterprise. It's Darwinian survival of the fittest. And I'm fit. My God, am I fit.

He flexes his muscles.

FRANCES: How much did you pay for that? We're penniless.

BETHUNE: You mean we've spent all your money? Never mind. Your true love and hero will open an office smack dab in the centre of Detroit. We'll paper the walls with money. And the ceiling and the floors.

The PORTER takes their bags and exits, followed by BETHUNE and FRANCES.

Scene 2

FRANCES enters holding a urine sample. She holds it at arm's length. BETHUNE enters.

BETHUNE: *with a Scottish accent*   How's my wee nurse?   *He reaches for a bottle of Scotch.*   A wee drop o' Scotch.

He holds it as if he's about to gulp it down.

FRANCES: Miss Scarlet's sample.

BETHUNE: *musing*   Miss Scarlet — that's her name this month, is it? Come on, Frances. Look, it's only urine. All us poor mortals piss, you know. Except you, of course. You're different, you're made of marble — not corruptible flesh like the rest of us.

FRANCES: And what does that mean?

There is a pause.

BETHUNE: You know.

FRANCES: Oh, God. Must we serve it up in working
    hours too?

BETHUNE: Reserved for bedtime only, is it?

FRANCES: Stop.

BETHUNE: Everytime I see you walk toward me . . .

FRANCES: Beth, I'm sorry . . . give me time.

BETHUNE: How much time do you need? You had
    months in Europe. . . . Even had the King of Moravia's
    bed in Vienna.

FRANCES: *chastely*   You think the honeymoon was
    a fiasco.

BETHUNE: Don't you?

FRANCES: No. It was wonderful.

BETHUNE: Wonderful. If you get your "charlies"
    watching me sizzle.

FRANCES: I can't help it. With time. It's my background.

BETHUNE: *whispering*   Soon you'll be telling me you
    were raped by the game keeper at ten years of age.

FRANCES: Stop it.

BETHUNE: Is handling urine just too intimate, nurse?
    Nurse?

FRANCES: *screaming*   I'm-not-a-nurse.   *Beat.*
    I'm a . . . a . . .

BETHUNE pastes a label on the sample.

BETHUNE: A what? An aristocrat? Even aristocrats have normal bodily functions. Frances, prepare yourself for a shock. Every member of the Royal Family shits.

FRANCES: Stop!

BETHUNE: Without exception. Everyone of them. They urinate, defecate, copulate, and some have even been know to ...   *He whispers.*   ... masturbate.

He grabs her.

FRANCES: Stop it!

She holds back the tears.

BETHUNE: *softly*   Frances.

FRANCES: I can't take it. I can't. I'm sorry, but I can't. I don't belong in your new world. It's dirty. The streets are dirty and the people are dirtier. What good has it done me? We're as penniless as the day we got here. If the butcher didn't pay his bills with meat and the grocer with vegetables, we wouldn't eat. The only people who pay are people like Miss Scarlet.

BETHUNE: She's in a hazardous profession. Look, cheer up. Take the sample and put it with the rest. Be careful, our Miss Scarlet has syphilis.

FRANCES pulls her hand away and covers her face.

BETHUNE: *laughing and moving to her*   Frances, Frances. Love, I can't help it if, when I looked at the map of Detroit and picked a street at its very centre, it would turn out to be a red light district. We'll make it. We will. Honestly. You'll look back and laugh at these days. Come on.

FRANCES: No. *She pulls back.*   Oh, it's not the grime of even the people. It's you. You're probably one of the most qualified surgeons in this city. London, Edinburgh, Vienna. Fellow of the Royal College of Surgeons. But here you rot . . . and I rot. If you were only practising surgery, instead of playing Dr. Livingstone in this putrid jungle.

BETHUNE: What do you want me to do? Crawl back to Edinburgh and beg "Daddy" to peddle his influence to get me a plum plucking the local blue bloods' pubies? I'd rather "dose up" Miss Scarlet.

FRANCES: Why must you always lace every word with blood? Talk in headlines like a tabloid? What hurts me is perfectly reasonable. Why aren't you practising surgery at the hospital for instance? Why?

BETHUNE: You have to be invited. I haven't been invited.

FRANCES: Oh, forgive me. The director hasn't come to our grimy little doorway, hat in hand, with a gilded invitation.

BETHUNE: What do you want? You know. You're the surgeon with your small white hands, your proper manners and crystal tears. You've got the knife and you're gently trying to deball me! I don't need to grovel, pull strings or smile at cocktail parties to make it. I can do it alone. I can. I will!

FRANCES: I. I. I. What about us?

BETHUNE: Everything I do is for us.

FRANCES: Everything is for you. You. Norman Bethune. Man of destiny. "God has laid his hands on this boy." I've heard your mother talk.

BETHUNE: Leave my mother out of this.

16

FRANCES: Then leave mine out. And my father and my uncles. You resent them because they don't agree with you. The infallible Bethune!

BETHUNE: I resent them because they have made the world stop turning. Everything is in its inscrutable, implacable passionless place. Why? Because they like it that way. It's comfortable and tidy and they run it. And if you don't drink their tea and eat their cucumber sandwiches and genuflect at their titles, you're banished. You hate the new world because you have to break the sod for your own garden. There's not some miserable moron servant to dirty his hands for you! Like his father did and his father before him. Grovelling for your inbred, imbecilic little society.

FRANCES: Oh, you fake! You hypocrite! You love silk sheets and champagne more than they do. You love money and service and first class cabins. If you don't support their system, why drink their wine?

BETHUNE: *softly* You turn my stomach. You sickening, dumb debutante. Oozing with grace and cricket morality. Don't you see? It's not the champagne or silk sheets. It's the exclusion, debarment, the lockout that goes with it. Because I like rolling, doesn't mean I go for your little system. There is no connection!

FRANCES: I want to go home!

BETHUNE: What?

FRANCES: I said, I want to go home!

BETHUNE: Home!

FRANCES: Yes, home.

BETHUNE: Ah!

FRANCES: I do. I'm sorry.

BETHUNE: Father will be so pleased. How he'll gloat.
Quoting him in a Scottish accent.   "You've made a
very sensible decision, my dear. That rude, awful man
would only destroy you. Sit down. Take some tea."
Beat.   Go! Go. Go. You have my blessing.   *Pause.*
I hope your father's hemorrhoids burst with pride.

There is a pause.

FRANCES: What will you do?

BETHUNE: Marry Miss Scarlet.

FRANCES: I'm serious.

BETHUNE: So am I. We'll have a beautiful spiritual
relationship. The physical side being a bit dodgy at
present.

FRANCES: Oh, why?

BETHUNE: Why, what?

There is a pause.

FRANCES: Why do I!

BETHUNE: Why do you love me?   *Beat.*   You love
me for the same reason a two foot, ninety pound runt
drives a million horse-power motorbike. It gives you
balls. It saves you from pinching yourself during your
delicate little days to see if you're still here. That's why.
Pause.   Frances, you're a fool . . . I thought you
were leaving.

FRANCES: I've changed my mind.

BETHUNE: *relieved*   Frances, your feet stink and you
don't love Jesus. End of drama. Where's my cigarettes?

FRANCES: There's one behind your ear.

18

BETHUNE: Ta. *Lighting up.* Frances, don't get so shell-shocked by everything. I had to start somewhere. Things will pick up.

FRANCES: Beth. Would you see him?

BETHUNE: Who?

FRANCES: The director . . . if you met him?

BETHUNE: What director?

FRANCES: The director of the hospital.

BETHUNE: If I met him? I'd have to see him. Of course, I could close my eyes. I could crouch behind the sofa.

FRANCES: Beth. Would you mention . . . about yourself . . . about your work . . . would you?

BETHUNE: If he asked, I suppose.

FRANCES: Would you see him this afternoon?

BETHUNE: What have you been up to?

FRANCES: Nothing . . . nothing really. He expects to see you in his office at four o'clock.

BETHUNE: Frances! You conniving bitch. Oh God, how that little mind works.

FRANCES: You said you were taking over the samples to the state laboratory there, so I . . . I talked to the director . . . I thought . . .

BETHUNE: You thought. Thought what? I'd drop in a few gallons of urine and then conveniently go up a few floors, hat in hand.

FRANCES: You said yourself the operation on Mrs. Rafferty's leg was done by a butcher. If you were there, that wouldn't have happened. You said it.

BETHUNE: Oh God, you're clever. It's Mrs. Rafferty's leg I'm crusading for with my wide smile, drooping tail and fat curriculum vitae to let him wipe his ass with.

FRANCES: He seemed very reasonable.

BETHUNE: So was God when he gave us the Ten Commandments. You have to be invited.

FRANCES: He said he'd be delighted to meet you.

BETHUNE: Very well, dear, I'll go. He's so reasonable. Nothing like "Daddy." I mean, he won't mind if I don't wear my black suit and stiff collar. Of course not. He wouldn't be put off by that. He's no stuffed shirt. Let's see, I'll wear this.   *He puts on a garish jacket.* That will put him at ease. Then there's the trousers. *He points to the trousers that he is wearing.*   Yes . . . *He clips on a hideous bow tie.*   As you say, he'll be perfectly reasonable. Well. Can't be late for my appointment. Urine samples, ah . . . my curriculum vitae. I'm off. I'm so glad he's so reasonable.

BETHUNE exits.

Scene 3

BETHUNE: *banging*   Shop!

A MATRON enters. She is sullen and officious. BETHUNE smiles at her, but she is unmoved.

MATRON: Yes!

BETHUNE: Yes.

MATRON: Yes.

BETHUNE: Yes.

MATRON: Yes!

BETHUNE: Hmm. I have an appointment with the director.

MATRON: Are you sure?

BETHUNE: No, I'm not sure. My wife made it.

MATRON: Your wife.

She looks critically at his clothes.

BETHUNE: Yes, I think she's my wife. I married her anyway.

MATRON: Are you sure you're not a salesman? We have rules about drug salesmen.

BETHUNE: No, I'm not a salesman. I'm an African missionary actually. Are you saved?

MATRON: Pardon me?

BETHUNE: I said, are you saved? That's my job, saving people. I just thought I'd check you out.

MATRON: What did you say your name was?

BETHUNE: I don't believe I did. We haven't been formally introduced. It's Bethune.

The MATRON checks her list.

MATRON: Dr. Norman Bethune?

BETHUNE: Yes.

MATRON: Why didn't you tell me you are a doctor, Doctor?

BETHUNE: You didn't tell you were a nurse, Nurse.

MATRON: It just states surgeon here, Doctor. Any particular specialization?

BETHUNE: Landscaping.

MATRON;   Pardon.

BETHUNE: Landscaping. I'm sort of a surgical landscaper. It's a rare form of specialization. There was not much call for it in the Congo.

MATRON: I don't think I understand. What should I put down under specialization?

BETHUNE: Breasts.

MATRON: Pardon me.

BETHUNE: Breasts. I landscape breasts. Take yours for instance.

MATRON: Mine!

BETHUNE: Yes, yours. Don't be alarmed. Your breasts. I speak medically. They're relatively good breasts. However, on close examination, one appears to be larger than the other.

MATRON: Oh . . .

BETHUNE: As I say, don't be alarmed. This is fairly normal. However . . .

MATRON: What!

BETHUNE: Allow me.

He feels her breasts.

MATRON: But Doctor . . .

BETHUNE: Hmmmmmmmmmm . . .

MATRON: The director. Please wait here for the director.

BETHUNE: Oh . . . Hmmm. Very well.

The MATRON exits.

ASSISTANT DIRECTOR: Dr. Bethune.

He holds out his hand.

BETHUNE: *shaking his hand*   Good afternoon. I'm
    here on behalf of Mrs. Rafferty's leg. She had it operated
    on Wednesday. It is severely ulcerated and broken.
    Whoever did the job was a butcher. The lady in question
    is a patient of mine. I'm particularly interested in her
    case, as her husband pays his bills in groceries. Something
    I can't afford to overlook. I believe I could have done
    considerably better. I am a fellow of the Royal College
    of Surgeons and I've done post-graduate work in surgery
    in London, Edinburgh and Vienna, although as yet not
    been given visiting privileges at your hospital. Something
    I hoped you could remedy.

ASSISTANT DIRECTOR: I am sorry, Doctor. I am not
    the director. I am his executive assistant. The director has
    been called away suddenly and was unable to see you.
    He sends his apologies. Good day.

BETHUNE: *flabbergasted, throwing his hat on the floor*
    Mission accomplished!

Scene 4

BETHUNE: I've just been "dumped on" from a great
    height. Well, what are you smiling at?

FRANCES: The director phoned. He read your
    curriculum vitae and would be delighted to open the
    facilities of the hopsital to you. Presto.

BETHUNE: Well, whoopee. Get back on the phone to him and tell him I want an operating room tomorrow morning. Then call Mrs. Rafferty. I want her there at seven o'clock. Tell her old man it will cost him a head of cabbage and a pound of carrots. I want to reset that leg before it's too late. Also, get the name of the hatchet man who did the job on her. I'd like a chat with him. Is there anybody outside?

FRANCES: Just one. It's that Miss Scarlet.

BETHUNE: Oh, hell.

FRANCES: What?

BETHUNE: What! How do I tell her?

FRANCES: Tell her what? She's got . . .

BETHUNE: You can say it, Frances. Syphilis.

FRANCES: I thought you said syphilis can be cured.

BETHUNE: There's no cure for her. It's too late. The damage has been done. It's irreversible. She's going to lose her sight completely and there's nothing I or anyone else can do about it *Beat.* Better ask her in.

FRANCES: *offstage* Come in please.

MISS SCARLET enters.

BETHUNE: Hello.

MISS SCARLET: Hi.

BETHUNE: Don't take your coat off.

MISS SCARLET: Uh?

BETHUNE: Do you like ice cream?

24

MISS SCARLET: Sure, why?

BETHUNE: Well, I adore ice cream and it's hot. Let's walk
    down to Kelly's and get some. I'll treat, since you're my
    one and only faithful customer today. What do you say?

MISS SCARLET: *unsure*   Okay.

BETHUNE: *putting on his coat*   I'd ask Nurse, but ice
    cream turns her hair green and makes her teeth drop out.

MISS SCARLET: Yeh?

BETHUNE: Not really, but someone has to mind the
    shop. Come on, we can talk on the way.

Scene 5

*BETHUNE takes out what appears to be a large canvas
wrapped in brown paper. He unwraps it and sets it on an
easel. He opens his paints, selects some brushes, etc. . . .
FRANCES enters.*

BETHUNE: What?

FRANCES: What do you mean, what?

BETHUNE: What do you want? I'm busy.

FRANCES: Oh. Our painting stint.

BETHUNE: What are you talking about?

FRANCES: You know what I'm talking about.

BETHUNE: Don't start.

FRANCES: Beth, what's wrong?

BETHUNE: Nothing's wrong.

FRANCES: Why are you painting?

BETHUNE: There's no customers, so I'm filling in my time with a useful pursuit. You could do likewise. Go out in the garden and eat worms.

FRANCES: Why do you get like this?

BETHUNE: Like what?

FRANCES: Beth, what's the matter?

BETHUNE: Ochre. I think ochre is the answer.

FRANCES: You're painting. You paint when you're depressed.

BETHUNE: Nonsense. I paint because I like it. Do you mind?

FRANCES: When you're depressed.

BETHUNE: Frances, you're becoming redundant.

FRANCES: At least tell me what's depressing you? Dear God, I thought you'd be elated with the hospital appointment and all. But no, you're painting.

BETHUNE: Frances, I don't know where you dreamed up this ridiculous theory that I only paint when I'm depressed.

FRANCES: It's true.

BETHUNE: Rubbish. Anyway, you play the piano when you're depressed.

FRANCES: That's nonsense.

BETHUNE: Your mother told me. She said, "Frances always plays the piano when she's feeling down." She told me you played ten hours a day after you met me.

FRANCES: *giggling* Oh, Beth. *She sits down.*
You're feeling down about that prostitute, aren't you?

BETHUNE: The way you say prostitute comes out like parasol or pillow or marmalade. Like something inanimate, unimportant.

FRANCES: You're depressed because you can't do anything. That's why, isn't it? *Pause.* Beth?

BETHUNE: Um.

FRANCES: That's why. *Beat.* Darling, you shouldn't get so involved. You've done all you can. All anyone can. It's just the way the world turns.

BETHUNE: Soon you'll be telling me the poor will always be with us.

FRANCES: Maybe it's true. They always have been.

BETHUNE: Ah, the primrose-scented oracle speaks.

FRANCES: Well, if she'd get a decent job instead of what she did, she wouldn't have all this . . . this mess.

BETHUNE: Does she make you vomit?

FRANCES: Now stop.

BETHUNE: Not much sympathy for someone slowly being devoured by all those itsy, syphilitic creepy-crawlies.

FRANCES: What are you painting?

BETHUNE: Nothing much. Just touching up an old one.

FRANCES: What's so special about Miss Scarlet? You've got through this at least one hundred times since you've been treating these people. It hasn't bothered you before. Anyway, tomorrow you'll be doing surgery again. You can forget it.

BETHUNE: Forget it, eh?

FRANCES: Please, Beth. *She is concerned.* This Miss Scarlet. What did she say? What happened? She was upset?

BETHUNE: She didn't wince. *Pause.* Just stared at me with those eyes. Those big painted, empty eyes.

FRANCES: Maybe it didn't sink in. The . . . the awfulness . . .

BETHUNE: It sank in.

FRANCES: Maybe she's retarded.

BETHUNE: Maybe.

FRANCES: Why get depressed about it?

BETHUNE: I'm not depressed, for Christ's sake. *Pause.* One time my father was preaching. Actually, he was the guest preacher at this great cathedral type monstrosity in Toronto. I remember, it was Easter. I think they invited father because he was a hell and brimstone type. Thought he might get through to the sinners. You know, the ones that only show up on special occasions like Christmas and Easter. Anyway, he got stuck into it, scaring the living daylights out of everyone. I was in the front row, as usual. Anyway, he got so fired up about the last trump, Judgment — "The Dead shall rise" and all that — that his false teeth sailed out of his mouth over the pulpit and landed with a clatter in the aisle. Did that disturb my father? Not at all. He kept preaching, gumming out the thunder. He just walked back around the pulpit, down the aisle, put back in his teeth and kept going. Didn't even miss a beat. I don't know if there were any converts, but God, did I laugh. I started and I couldn't stop. My mother had to take me outside. I think she thought it was pretty funny too, but she didn't let on. Anyway, that night my father gave me the thrashing of my life. *Pause.* Don't blame him really. I could see how he'd take it pretty hard, his son and all that. But then he did something I despised him for.

FRANCES passes him a rag.

BETHUNE: He came up to my room about two hours
     later. Weeping! Crying his eyes out, wringing his hands,
     and then . . . and then . . . he got on his knees, his knees!
     And begged me to forgive him.   *Pause.*   I thought I
     was going to vomit.   *Pause.*   I was about twelve at
     the time.

There is a pause.

FRANCES: All very touching. What does it all mean?

BETHUNE: *quietly*   It means Miss Scarlet doesn't make
     me vomit.   *He steps back from the painting, saying
     critically . . .*   Voilà!

He turns the painting around.

FRANCES: *speechless*   Oh . . . oh . . . oh . . .   *She
     stamps her feet.*   How could you? Beth, how could you
     do it? How? You said you were touching up one of your
     old paintings.

BETHUNE: I said no such thing. Touching up an old
     painting. Not necessarily mine.

FRANCES: It's the most valuable painting we have. An
     original French Impressionist that you paid 1200 francs
     we couldn't afford for. Now you've ruined it. It's
     worthless.

BETHUNE: Nonsense. I improved it. It needed the ochre.

FRANCES: You're mad. You're a madman.   *She
     looks at the painting.*   Ohhhhh . . .

She sobs.

BETHUNE: Now, Frances.

FRANCES: Why, why, why do you do these things?

BETHUNE: Don't get so upset. Anyway, it was a fake.

FRANCES: A fake?

BETHUNE: Yes. I knew when I bought it, it was a fake.

FRANCES: Then why did you buy it?

BETHUNE: It was irresistible. That funny little man at
            the Pont Marie put on such a great performance. I think
            he knew that I knew it was a fake. That performance was
            worth more than any original French Impressionist.

FRANCES: You are mad, aren't you?

BETHUNE: Cheer up. It's worth hanging on the wall now.

FRANCES continues to sob.

BETHUNE: Oh, hell. Go and play the piano. Touch up
            a bit of Beethoven, if it helps. I won't mind.

Scene 6

*FRANCES is setting a small table. She has a bottle of
champagne in an ice bucket. She places a small crystal vase
in the centre of the table and carefully arranges a large
rose and some ferns in it. BETHUNE enters and takes off
his coat.*

FRANCES: How did it go?

BETHUNE: Fine. The leg is fine. Broke it and re-set it.
            Smooth as clockwork. Your friend the director came
            sniffing around to see the show. Believe he was suitably
            impressed.

FRANCES: Did you see Greely?

BETHUNE: Greely?

FRANCES: He's the fellow you said botched up the operation the first time.

BETHUNE: No. He doesn't come in on Tuesdays. God, the man should be defrocked. I told the director though. *Mischievously.* Incidentally, Miss Machiavellian Femme Fatale, I note the director is a little Scotch-git from Edinburgh, no less. Of course, that has nothing to do with our change of fortune.

He reaches for her. She slips away, moves around the table and pours him a drink.

FRANCES: Nothing. Champagne, Doctor?

BETHUNE: Aha!

FRANCES: A toast to my white knight.

BETHUNE: *laughing* God, Frances. Everyone thinks you're so delicate and demure. Underneath that graceful exterior lies a Madame Defarge. Is my head on your list or have I lost it already?

There is a knock at the door.

BETHUNE: Oh, hell. Go and see who it is, love. See if it can wait till morning.

FRANCES exits. She returns, a little perplexed.

FRANCES: Beth, it's that Dr. Greely. He doesn't look very happy.

BETHUNE: Aha, show him in — and stay. I don't want you to miss this.

FRANCES: No, I'd rather not.

BETHUNE: Frances, stay. Show·him in.

FRANCES exits and returns, followed by GREELY, an immaculately dressed man, hat in hand.

GREELY: *To FRANCES*   Thank you. Bethune, I
understand you spoke rather disparagingly to the director
about an unfortunate piece of surgery I did on one of
your patients.

BETHUNE: Correct. Greely, I don't know how you got
to be a doctor, but . . .

GREELY: *interrupting him*   I know exactly how you
feel, but I'm not interested. I've already heard it all
via the director.

BETHUNE: And you're here to pour oil on troubled
waters. Things get a bit hot for you at the shop?

GREELY: On the contrary. I don't give a damn what you
say, your word counts for nothing.

BETHUNE: Why did you come?

GREELY: The director sent me to try and help you.

BETHUNE: Help me, "ah so," I'm intrigued.

GREELY: You're also a greenhorn.

BETHUNE: Pardon.

GREELY: You're a greenhorn, a beginner, wet behind the
ears. A young player.

BETHUNE: Jesus, I could run rings around you . . .

FRANCES: Beth!

GREELY: Perhaps as a surgeon. Albeit, an unsuccessful
one. Or do my eyes deceive me?

BETHUNE: Look here.

GREELY: Bethune, will you listen? The director likes
you and would like to keep you on, but . . .

BETHUNE: But what? . . . No, I think I see. If I don't catch on to whatever I'm supposed to catch on to, I'm in a word — out.

GREELY: In a word.

BETHUNE: Well, you know what you can do with . . .

FRANCES: Beth!

GREELY: Bethune. Will you please attempt to be civil and listen?

FRANCES: Beth, please.

GREELY: At the hospital, we all try and work together. God knows our profession is demanding enough. Why make the atmosphere unpleasant?

BETHUNE: That's what I was doing, was it? Fouling up the atmosphere.

GREELY: Yes. We don't need it. Neither do you. Now, look, how old are you?

FRANCES: He's thirty-six.

GREELY: You're thirty-six and still playing Robin Hood. Highly commendable. But you're as poor as the miserable wretches who come to you off the breadlines. Don't misunderstand, we're not like the medical profession in the old country. We're not snobs. In America, we're businessmen. It sounds crass, but we have to be. Bethune, you're a good surgeon and you could be living like one. I see you acquired a taste for champagne. Excellent *He falters.* The director put forth a proposal. *Beat.* And on reflection . . . *He pauses.* To the point. I am willing to send you half my surgical cases. They're used to paying handsomely. In return, you will give me a consultant's fee for each one on each visit. Of course, you will reciprocate when you build up your own clientele. You can keep this office, but you must refurnish it appropriately. You can still play Robin Hood if you like. I do myself. That's why I took that unfortunate woman. I never billed her or didn't she tell you, and I'm sorry it wasn't a satisfactory job. Now, if you need money, go and see my bank manager. He'll advance you whatever you require. Here's his card and mine. If the message has got through to you, fine. Phone me tomorrow. Now I must go. My wife is waiting for me in the car. Good evening. *Beat.* Mrs. Bethune. *Beat.* I'll show myself out. Good night.

BETHUNE sits silently.

FRANCES: Have some.

BETHUNE pours some champagne quickly and throws it back like brandy. He wanders to the window.

BETHUNE: There he goes "tootling" off in his Caddy. God Almighty.

FRANCES: America must be the only place ever to have achieved decadence without civilization.

BETHUNE: What's the difference? In your civilized bailiwick, they trade with titles and gilded invitations. Here, they deal in straight cash. It's quite refreshing really. *Pause.* God, they don't teach this in Berlin or Vienna or London or all the other institutions I've been flushed through.

There is a pause.

FRANCES: Beth. *Beat.* Be sensible.

BETHUNE: Oh, he's right, of course. So are you. God, I'm a fool. *Beat.* "Robin Hood." *Pause.* Let's celebrate. Make a list of all the things your little heart desires. We'll paper the walls with money yet.

FRANCES leans over and gently kisses him.

Scene 7

FRANCES: And finally, this is the living room.

FIRST FRIEND: It's so comfortable. What kind of chairs are those?

FRANCES: Tudor. My father shipped them to us from Edinburgh. They have sat in our ancestral home for three hundred years. The framed tartan over the fireplace is also very old. My great great grandfather's regimental tartan. He led the Highland Brigade at Balaclava. All the rest, as you can see, is quite modern.

SECOND FRIEND: You've made it blend so beautifully.

FRANCES: Thank you, please sit down.

SECOND FRIEND: Where's Norm?

FRANCES: I don't know. He promised to be home early, but he's been so busy. I worry about him. He's still got that awful cold and he's lost weight, but he won't take a holiday.

SECOND FRIEND: He's getting to be the most eminent surgeon in Detroit.

FIRST FRIEND: Such a delightful custom. A house-warming.

FRANCES: We wanted it to be an intimate affair. I'm so pleased you could come. You must be very busy.

SECOND FRIEND: Wouldn't have missed it. I'm so glad Norman's done so well. He deserves it.

FRANCES: Aperitif!

BETHUNE enters and places some X-rays on the coffee table.

GREELY: Ah, Norman.

BETHUNE: Hello, Greely. Good evening all. Sorry I'm
    late, dear. I've been drinking with old Rafferty. You
    remember, the grocer. He was my first client. Used to
    pay his bills with groceries too. He got me into his
    homemade wine. Makes it from the loose grapes in the
    bottom of the crates. Ingenious, don't you think?
    He grabs a cocktail.   Frances shown you her castle,
    has she?

FIRST FRIEND: It's beautiful.

BETHUNE: Yes, it looks like God himself built it. But
    I doubt if God could afford it.   *He looks around.*
    No doubt, showed you the regimental tartan. Her great
    grandmother or someone led the retreat at Balaclava.
    "Daddy" has his underwear made of it.

FRANCES: *picking up the dinner bell*   We'll be eating
    shortly.

BETHUNE: *taking the bell*   Before you eat, I'd like to
    tell you all a little story. Very appropriate for the occasion.

He coughs heavily. FRANCES goes to him.

BETHUNE: Alright. It's alright. Now, my story. Actually,
    it's a drama. A piece of theatre I've contrived for your
    amusement. It's called "The Story of Wee Willie Winky and
    the White Mouse."

FRANCES: Beth, please . . .

BETHUNE: Don't worry love, it's not dirty. Perhaps a little
    obscene, but not dirty. It seems Wee Willie Winky fell in
    love with this beautiful white mouse. He met her at a
    cricket game actually. Her hobby was keeping the score at
    cricket games. Not her hobby actually, her profession.
    Her whole family made a fortune this way, at the cricket
    games. I'm sorry, you don't know what cricket is?

FIRST FRIEND: I've heard of it.

BETHUNE: It's a polite game where you clap your
opponents very sportingly, even if they're thrashing the
ass off you, then you all drink tea. Marvellous game.
Anyway, Wee Willie married the cricketing white mouse
and they went on their honeymoon swinging on pendulums.
Oh, pendulums all over the place. The Riviera, Vienna —
just everywhere. The white mouse paid for it because she
was rich, but one day they woke up to find all their money
was gone. Never mind, said Wee Willie, I've heard of a land
inhabited by rich mechanical mice and since I'm a rather
clever mechanic, I'll go and set up a shop there fixing the
mechanical mice's clockwork when it starts to run down.
And so he did. But he had a problem. The place where he
set up his workshop was in the mechanical mice's
playground. The mechanical mice played a funny game.
Actually, it was a silly game. At least, the white mouse
thought so. Not nearly as good as cricket. Anyway, this
game was called "getting your oil changed." It was run
by the little girl mechanical mice. But it could be dangerous.
There was always the danger the little girlie mechanical mice
could get their carburetors fouled up and the little boys
their pistons scored. Willie found himself busy trying to
fix this, but it was hard and then they wouldn't pay their
bills. Also, the white mouse was unhappy, she missed the
huge cheese castle she used to live in and she missed the
cricket games. But thanks to the white mouse, he found a
solution and made lots of money by embarking on a life
of crime. It was really simple, you just convinced the
healthy mechanical mice they were sick, then you could
cure them and cure them and cure them forever. Sometimes
he'd let his friends cure them too, so they all made lots of
money. Everybody was very happy. The white mouse could
play cricket again by teaching some of Wee Willie's new
friends the game, and also, Wee Willie brought her a bigger
cheese castle than she'd ever had. Well, everything would
have turned out fine, but poor Willie Winkie had been
working so long with the oil change casualties that the
fumes swallowed so long ago started to eat him up inside.
So he had to walk around with a bell . . .   *He rings the
bell.*   . . . Calling.   *Speaking softly.*   Unclean.
Unclean. Unclean.

*BETHUNE becomes hoarse, then breaks into an intense
coughing spasm. FRANCES and the FIRST FRIEND help
BETHUNE out. GREELY follows. The SECOND FRIEND
goes immediately to the X-ray envelope and examines the
X-ray.*

SECOND FRIEND: My God! Greely, come here!

There is a pause.

GREELY: Is it Beth's?

SECOND FRIEND: I'm afraid so.   *Beat.*   Pulmonary
     tuberculosis. Look.   *Beat.*   Cavenous! Already
     spreading to the right lung, by the look of it.

GREELY: You're the expert. How bad is it?

SECOND FRIEND: *pausing, then slowly shaking his head*
     Go and get Frances, will you?   *Beat.*   We'll have to
     get him to a sanitorium immediately.

Scene 8

*MCKENNA is pacing back and forth, looking at his watch.
He is nervous.*

NURSE: This way please. The director will see you now.

MCKENNA: Ah. Mrs. Bethune, delighted.   *He shakes
     hands with her.*   Please sit down.

FRANCES: *worried*   You wanted to see me. What's
     wrong, where's Beth?

MCKENNA: He's coming. Just wanted to meet you . . .
     before you talk to your husband, that is.

FRANCES: There is something wrong.

MCKENNA: Not at all. Please relax.

FRANCES: Then, why? I know his condition.

MCKENNA: Please, Mrs. Bethune. Your husband has been in our sanatorium quite some time. This is your first visit. That's your business, of course. No, I just wanted to bring you up to date, so to speak. That's all.

FRANCES: Up to date, on what? Is it much worse?

MCKENNA: Nothing to be alarmed at. No, I wanted to bring you up to date on your husband's . . . on Dr. Bethune's . . . activities.

FRANCES: Activities!

MCKENNA: Activities. He's an active man, in spite of his condition. Sanatoriums are supposed to be places of inactivity, you know.

FRANCES: I know.

MCKENNA: Of course, everyone is fond of your husband. Staff and patients alike. He's popular. I'm very fond of him myself. He bends the rules a little. Like sneaking into town to Brooke's tavern!

FRANCES: I'm not surprised.

MCKENNA: Of course not. Then there's his painting.

FRANCES: *quietly*   He paints.

MCKENNA: Yes, and so quickly. Covers a canvas in no time, they tell me. Case in point, his mural . . .

FRANCES: Mural.

MCKENNA: Mural. One night while the rest of the patients
slept, he covered all the walls in his ward with a mural.
All of them, yes, all four walls, in one night! Not discovered
till morning. Brightens up the ward, I suppose, and not
without artistic merit. Patients won't hear of it being
removed. The last panel of the mural is in questionable
taste, I think. The angel of death carrying off your husband
after he has been lured onto the rocks by the sirens of
success and wealth. Carrying him off over the churchyard
into a starlit sky. Yes, and underneath this sort of doggerel
verse:

"Sweet death, thou kindest Angel of them all,
In thy soft arms at last, O, let me fall,
Bright stars are out. Long gone the burning sun,
My little act is over, and the tiresome play is done."

In the churchyard, he has all the tombs clearly marked,
not only his own, but all the other patients in the ward,
with the projected dates of their deaths on them.
Questionable. Of course, everyone took it in the right
spirit. We tried to give him a useful outlet for his energy.
Let him give lectures to the nurses on anatomy. Very
good too. His last lecture on the male anatomy was
unfortunate. Mischievously visual.   *He clears his
throat. He has forgotten FRANCES' presence in the
room, and he rambles on.*   I have considerable
affection for him. He did present me with a beautiful
gift at Christmas. Beautiful. A travelling bag. English
leather, I'm told. Yes, loves a joke. Imitates me doing
my rounds. All in good fun, I suppose. Gives his own
diagnosis. Often directly the opposite to mine. In fun,
I'm sure. Some of his recommended treatments in these
mock rounds perhaps go a bit far. Recommended suicide,
for instance. Mind you, he's liked, as you Britishers say,
he's a wag.   *Grimly.*   A wag.

FRANCES: Please. I realize he must be a trying patient.
. . . He was a trying husband. I'm here to say goodbye!

MCKENNA: Goodbye.

FRANCES: I leave for Scotland tomorrow. Our divorce is final.

MCKENNA: Divorce.

FRANCES: *matter of factly* Beth insisted on it, and I couldn't take anymore . . . So . . .

MCKENNA: I see.

FRANCES: Doctor, why do you want to see me?

MCKENNA: It's this latest idea he has.

FRANCES: Oh!

MCKENNA: He wants artificial pneumothorax, something he discovered in some medical journal. An operation which is still highly experimental and risky in my opinion. What happens is: air is pumped into the chest cavity of the diseased lung by a hollow needle inserted between the ribs. Theoretically, the treatment is sound. The diseased lung, if collapsed, becomes inoperative, allowing the infected area to rest and heal itself, so to speak. However, there is grave danger of the needle puncturing the lung, which could lead to fatal complications! It's a kind of kill or cure situation I don't approve of. Your husband hasn't given thorough bed-rest a chance. Two more years of complete bed-rest could have very positive results.

FRANCES: What's this got to do with me?

MCKENNA: Your husband is very persistent. *Beat.* Persuasive. He's slowly winning over some of the younger members of my staff. If the operation is carried out and the results are unfortunate, I do not want repercussions from his next of kin. However, in the light of his new marital situation . . . this would seem to be . . . Mrs. Beth . . .

BETHUNE: *offstage* McKenna! Are you in there?

41

NURSE: *offstage*   Please . . . you can't!

BETHUNE: What do you mean, I can't! The little bastard
has managed to dodge me all day. McKenna!   *He bursts*
in.   There you are. Earl Warren has agreed to operate
Tuesday, if he gets the go ahead. And he's a staff man, so
now what's your excuse?   *He sees FRANCES.*   Who's
your friend?

FRANCES and BETHUNE stare at each other. FRANCES
slowly rises. Meanwhile, MCKENNA tries to tiptoe out the
door.

BETHUNE: Where are you going? Sneaky bastard! I
want an answer!

MCKENNA: We will decide at the staff meeting at three
o'clock.

BETHUNE: Three o'clock. I'll be there. Here, here's a
list of books for the library. Take it with you.

MCKENNA is embarrassed. He takes the list and exits
quickly.

BETHUNE: *to FRANCES*   I thought we'd agreed
you'd never come here.

FRANCES: I sail tomorrow. The divorce is final.

There is silence.

BETHUNE: Where is it?

FRANCES takes a piece of paper out of her purse.
BETHUNE slowly takes it and reads it. He coughs.
FRANCES helps him to a chair. He is visibly shaken.

BETHUNE: Ha!   *Attempting to be jocular.*   It says
here I have to pay you over $26,000 in alimony.
Congratulations. You're rich.   *Beat.*   I'm penniless,
so marry me.

FRANCES: Beth . . .

They stare at each other, then she rushes to him. They cling to each other.

BETHUNE: I'll walk you to the gate.

They exit. For the first time in the play, his voice cracks a little.

ACT TWO

Scene 1

FRANCES is playing the piano. BRIGIT enters with a traymobile, followed by FRANCES' MOTHER and FATHER. Her FATHER is carrying a newspaper. FRANCES continues to play the piano. Her FATHER reads his newspaper. Her MOTHER goes to FRANCES and closes the keyboard.

MOTHER: Thank you, Brigit. I'll pour.

BRIGIT exits. FRANCES takes some tea and sits down silently.

MOTHER: You tea's ready, Father.

FATHER: *lowering his newspaper*   Oh. Aye.   *He continues to read.*   Whoever invented the modern highway was a menace.

MOTHER: I believe it was a Scot, dear.   *She thinks about it.*   McAdam.

FATHER: Built a car you can buy for 100 pounds. Everyone and his uncle will own one now. Where will it end?

MOTHER: Highways are not the menace. It's the cars.

FATHER: It's highways. Without highways, what's the use of cars? I agree with the Duke of Wellington. He was against the building of public roads, said it encourages the masses to move about needlessly.   *Pause.*   It's these Socialists. They're ruining the country.

MOTHER: What do you think, Frances?

FRANCES: Pardon?

MOTHER: Never mind.

Her FATHER continues to read.

FATHER: This McAdam should've been hung.

MOTHER: Hanged, I think you mean. People are hanged, not hung.

FATHER: Believe it's hung.

MOTHER: Hanged! Hanged, not hung. Frances?

FRANCES: I don't know, Mother. I dare say, the correct pronunciation would mean little if you were going to the gallows.

FATHER: Hung then.

There is a pause.

MOTHER: *to FRANCES*   Would you like to go to the flower show? It's very good this year, I believe.

FRANCES: Flowers. No thank you.

MOTHER: Frances, you've been home a week and you haven't stirred from this room. You've had a terrible time of it, but life must go on. Isn't that so, Father?

FATHER: *wrapped up in his newspaper* Aye.

MOTHER: What is it, Brigit?

BRIGIT: *entering excitedly* The post. For Miss Frances.

MOTHER: Well.

BRIGIT produces the mail from her pocket. FRANCES seizes it.

MOTHER: *icily* How many times have I told you, bring the post in on a tray. Never handle anything with your bare hands. Goodness gracious, girl, your mother was in service. Didn't she tell you that? *She motions BRIGIT out, and speaks softly to FRANCES.* Frances.

FRANCES: Please, I'd like to be alone.

MOTHER: Dear . . .

FATHER: Come on, Mother.

FRANCES reads from a letter. BETHUNE appears on the edge of the scene.

FRANCES: The operation was short and a complete success. It's incredible.

BETHUNE: I took my last walk around the sanitorium today. Here they lay — so many of them — dying by degrees. Prisoners. Useless. Afraid. And I'm walking out of the gates, thanks to some simple surgery they won't get unless they break down the walls like I did. I swear, I'll do something about it. I go from here to Ray Brook Hospital in New York for a course in bacteriology. Then to Montreal to the Royal Victoria Hospital as a thoracic surgeon, to work under Edward Archibald, the most eminent man in the field in North America. For the first time in my life, there seems to be a meaningful pattern to my existence. *Pause.* I . . . I . . . think about you a lot . . . Frances . . . write.

BETHUNE exits.

MOTHER: *offstage* Frances . . . are you alright?

FRANCES: *rising* I'm fine. *Beat.* What did you say about a flower show?

She exits.

Scene 2

ARCHIBALD enters with the hospital ACCOUNTANT, MATRON and DIRECTOR. They march in. They all sit at once and cross their legs in unison.

ARCHIBALD: Is he here?

MATRON: Perhaps.

ARCHIBALD: What do you mean, Matron?

ACCOUNTANT: I think she means "perhaps," if that is the person in the turtleneck sweater . . .

MATRON: Trying to convince your secretary to go skiing with him . . .

ACCOUNTANT: "Perhaps," if that is the man . . .

DIRECTOR: It's him! He nearly ran me over in the parking lot in an open sports car! A vehicle, I might add, that has seen better days.

ACCOUNTANT: Sports car!

MATRON: Open! In mid-winter!

The DIRECTOR nods. They all nod, except ARCHIBALD.

ARCHIBALD: Ask him in.

DIRECTOR: Before you do, Doctor, we would like to bring up a few points before this man is appointed.

ARCHIBALD: Yes?

ACCOUNTANT: We have received a letter from a Dr. Greely in Detroit. Apparently, some of his professional behaviour is questionable.

DIRECTOR: Apparently this fellow Bethune sold his entire practice for a mere $5,000 to some youngster right out of medical school.

MATRON: Apparently this price included all his books and furniture.

ACCOUNTANT: Apparently, all done without informing his partner.

DIRECTOR: Unethical.

ACCOUNTANT: Questionable.

MATRON: Apparently.

The Trio nod.

ARCHIBALD: I have engaged a surgeon, not a priest. The letter I received from the director of Ray Brook Hospital says Bethune learned more in bacteriology in three months than most people learn in three years.

MATRON: The letter also says he is a "Saint Catherine's wheel." .

ACCOUNTANT: With energy going in all directions.

DIRECTOR: We read the letter.

ARCHIBALD: *patiently* Matron, please show Dr. Bethune in.

The MATRON goes to the door.

MATRON: *offstage* Dr. Bethune. *Beat.* Please.

When the MATRON leaves — the ACCOUNTANT and the DIRECTOR stand. When she returns, the Trio all sit and cross their legs in unison.

ARCHIBALD: *shaking BETHUNE's hand.* Welcome to Montréal. This is Matron, Director, Accountant.

BETHUNE: *nonchalantly* Hi.

ARCHIBALD: How do you feel?

BETHUNE: I suppose anyone who has been released from a sanatorium after two years feels the same. What-do-I-do-now kind of thing. Thirty-eight. Divorced. Broke and beginning a new career.

MATRON: Could have gone back to your practice in Detroit.

ACCOUNTANT: A successful practice from all accounts.

DIRECTOR: Which poses the question . . .

MATRON: Why leave a lucrative private practice and go into a field that is highly experimental? . . .

ACCOUNTANT: And poorly paid.

BETHUNE: *musing* My successful practice. *Beat.* Success is a whore. She will lead you on, then drop you.

ACCOUNTANT: Pardon!

The Trio exchange glances.

BETHUNE: The youth with fifty cents in his pocket about to see his girl is better off than the millionaire whose prostate is acting up.

The Trio clear their throats.

ARCHIBALD: How did things go at Ray Brook? I understand you worked under Bray himself.

BETHUNE: *reaching into his inner coat pocket*   Here is the report on my work in pseudo-TB in rats. Bray thought you might be interested.

ARCHIBALD: Ah. He wrote me. You took over the research project Smith and Wilson abandoned.   *He reads from the report.*   Lung collapse in albino rats . . . you achieved that! . . . What's this? . . .

BETHUNE: Nothing to do with it. Some changes I'd envisioned for the present artificial pneumothorax machine. I've reversed these valves here. The stopclock is higher and I've added a simple mechanism for drawing off fluid from the pleural cavity.

ARCHIBALD: What's this?

BETHUNE: A foot pump.

ARCHIBALD: *impressed*   You've given the whole thing a two-in-one function . . . ingenious.

BETHUNE: If it works.

ARCHIBALD: We'll see. I'll have Sid make up a working model. Is this something else?

BETHUNE: Rib shears. The ones we all use now are all-purpose. They're clumsy and inefficient for cutting into the rib cage. These simply sing through the ribs. They are not original, mind. Courtesy of the United Shoe Company. Shoemaker's shears. I've simply blunted the ends and extended the handles nine inches. They go through the rib cage like butter.

ARCHIBALD walks out, engrossed. BETHUNE follows.
The Trio give "miffed off" expressions in unison.

ARCHIBALD: Come and see the boys in the machine
shop. They'll be delighted.   *Handing over the rib*
shears.   Matron, scrub these up. I'd like to try them
tomorrow.

BETHUNE walks out after ARCHIBALD, but pauses to
speak to the distraught Trio.

BETHUNE: Are you all one unit? Or are the parts
interchangeable?

The Trio all rise in unison and march off in disgust.

Scene 3

FRANCES enters carrying a large box. She opens a layer of
wrapping paper and reads the letter in the envelope before
opening the box.

BETHUNE: *calling softly*   Frances . . . God, I miss you.
Wish you were here.   *Beat.*   Believe I've changed.
I don't want to snatch at you ever again. I want you to
be just Frances Penney, the Frances Penney I met in
Edinburgh so long ago — self-contained and undistorted.
Pause.   These are exciting times here. At last, it seems
we are making some headway. Thoracic surgery is now
common in most sanatoriums and hospitals. But the
battle has just begun. It has become increasingly evident
to many of us that, although we are succeeding as never
before in the operating theatre, we are losing ground to
the ambivalence and neglect in the political arena. By
the time we see the poor, the disease is usually well
advanced. They won't come earlier because they're afraid
they'll lose their jobs and be faced with a crippling
doctor's bill. Medical care should be free. Once a week,
a group — pitifully few from my own profession, I'm
afraid — plus laymen, writers, poets, painters and

ordinary concerned citizens meet at my apartment. We call ourselves the Montreal Group for the Security of the People's Health. We've drafted an outline for a reasonable state medical plan. I wish you could meet them. We are going to send the report to every level of government, every politician and every doctor. The doctors are important. We must convince them that they are in no danger of becoming puppets of the state. Well, here I am, rambling on. But it's exciting and I believe I've found myself in this fight. *Pause.* Frances, it's been two years. You say you are lonely. So am I. *Pause.* I've told you about my inventions, so I've sent you one.

She opens the parcel. It is an old-fashioned gramophone turntable. On the turntable are the figures of Wee Willie Winkie and the white mouse. When the gramophone is wound up, the figures waltz. It is really a large music box. FRANCES winds up the music box.

MOTHER: *entering* Frances, there you are . . . Gracious! What's that?

FRANCES: *delighted with the gift* Wee Willie Winkie and the white mouse. *Beat.* Dancing . . .

MOTHER: I suppose *he* sent it.

FRANCES: Yes.

MOTHER: He's persistent.

FRANCES: Where's Father?

MOTHER: Coming. Why?

FRANCES: I want to say goodbye.

MOTHER: You're not going to . . . ?

FRANCES: Yes, Mother.

FATHER: *entering* Not going to what . . . ?

FRANCES: I'm going to marry Beth again.

FATHER: You're a foolish girl.

FRANCES: Remember the day I married Beth? It was the thirteenth and I broke my hand mirror. Beth said, "Now I can make your life a misery . . . *Beat.* . . . but I'll never bore you."

MOTHER AND FATHER: *together* Frances. Don't . . .

They ad lib. FRANCES begins to waltz like the figures on the music box. She waltzes over to BETHUNE and they dance. Her MOTHER and FATHER exit, shaking their heads. The waltz ends.

Scene 4

BETHUNE takes FRANCES to the forestage area and gestures upstage.

BETHUNE: Welcome home.

FRANCES: It's magnificent.

BETHUNE: You like it?

FRANCES: *laughing* Daresay, these French Impressionists are not fakes.

BETHUNE: *laughing* No, they're not fakes.

FRANCES: And the Jacobean furniture.

BETHUNE: Even have a four-poster bed.

FRANCES: Your fortunes *have* certainly changed.

BETHUNE: My fortunes are still the same, I'm afraid.
Flat stoney broke.

FRANCES: *looking around*   But how . . .

BETHUNE: It's not mine. The apartment belongs to a
friend of mine, R.E. Coleman, rich, executive type.
Charming fellow. You'll like him.

FRANCES: But where is he?

BETHUNE: *looking at his watch*   Be home in one hour
and twelve minutes — he's very punctual.

FRANCES: You mean, he lives here too.

BETHUNE: No, we "live here too." It's his apartment.
Pause.   Now, don't get "funny" about it. It's only
for a short time.

FRANCES: A short time.

BETHUNE: Until we get the Medical Plan through.

FRANCES: Medical Plan! What's that got to do with it?

BETHUNE: Until then, I refused to bill anyone. I live off
my monthly hospital stipend. I can't point fingers at
the fee-for-service system if I'm living off it, can I?

FRANCES: Martyr for the cause.

BETHUNE: Now, Frances . . .

FRANCES: I'm supposed to be a martyr too. Living in
someone else's house. Why don't we do it properly and go
and live in a tenement?

BETHUNE: *exasperated*   Ahhh . . .

FRANCES: Thanks for telling me.

BETHUNE: I didn't think it was important.

FRANCES: Of course not.

BETHUNE: Come on, love. Things will pick up. You'll
look back . . .

FRANCES AND BETHUNE   *together*   And laugh at
these days.

FRANCES: I've heard it before. Remember.

BETHUNE: Christ, why don't you play the piano?
R.E. has got a baby grand. Just for you. Daresay, you'll
prefer it to the four-poster bed.

BETHUNE storms out.

Scene 5

*ARCHIBALD and the Trio re-enter. The Trio march in and
sit in unison, as before. ARCHIBALD follows at his own
pace.*

ARCHIBALD: Well?

*There is a pause. The MATRON and the ACCOUNTANT nod
at the DIRECTOR, who stands up.*

DIRECTOR: *sanctimoniously*   Doctor. After a lot of
soul-searching and discussion, we recommend you dismiss
Dr. Bethune.

ARCHIBALD: *incredulous*   Dismiss Bethune!

DIRECTOR: Dismiss him.

MATRON: Dismiss him!

ACCOUNTANT: He's a poseur.

MATRON: Immoral. A poor example.

DIRECTOR: Destructive, an iconoclast.

MATRON: He's destroying the clinic.

ACCOUNTANT: Dangerous.

DIRECTOR: He's ruining *your* life's work.

ARCHIBALD: Rubbish! Now, this is name-calling. Hardly sufficient to dismiss a man. You'll have to do better than that.

MATRON: Have you read this?

ACCOUNTANT: "Montreal Doctor Scorns Medical Profession."

DIRECTOR: *reading*   "Speaking to the Canadian Progress Club of Montreal, Dr. Norman Bethune conducted an imaginary investigation into the death of John Bunyan, a victim of tuberculosis. Acting as judge and jury, Bethune indicted the doctors who examined him, the doctors at the sanatorium for releasing him too soon and the government for allowing him to return to heavy work too soon – for his untimely death. Bethune said 'There is a rich man's tuberculosis and a poor man's tuberculosis; the rich man lives and the poor man dies.' He then delivered a list of suggestions, some of them most radical, to prevent similar deaths."   *He interrupts his reading.*   Radical is not the word!

MATRON: He advocates state medicine.

ACCOUNTANT: Look at this, "Montreal Doctor Shocks Medical Assembly." Listen!   *Reading.*   "Socialized medicine and the abolition of restriction of private practice would appear to be the realistic solution to the community health care problem. Let us take the profit, the private economic profit, out of medicine and purify our profession of rapacious individualism. Let us make it disgraceful to enrich ourselves at the expense of the miseries of our fellow men. Let us organize ourselves so that we can no longer be exploited by our politicians, or be held back by the King Canute of the Canadian Medical Association."

MATRON: Insulting!

DIRECTOR: Do you know how many outraged letters I got from the Minister?

ACCOUNTANT: If Bethune continues this business, all government funds will be cut off from the clinic.

MATRON: Then where will we be?

ARCHIBALD: Perhaps. But that is not sufficient reason to dismiss him. You're not fools. You know as well as I do, if Bethune is dismissed from this clinic, he will lose all credibility with his profession. No one will take his ideas seriously and any reforms he proposes will be rejected out of hand — by everyone!

MATRON: Surely you don't agree with his ideas!

ARCHIBALD: No, I don't. I think they're too radical. But I have no better ones. I'm not going to dismiss him because I don't agree with him. That would be senseless and destructive and iconoclastic and all the other names you've bandied around.

ACCOUNTANT: This man is disruptive to the clinic.

DIRECTOR: To the whole medical profession.

MATRON: And you won't dismiss him on any grounds?

ARCHIBALD: Not on the grounds you've put forward anyway.

DIRECTOR: What grounds do you think justify dismissal?

ARCHIBALD: If I found his or any other surgeon's work in this hospital destructive or incompetent, I'd dismiss him. But a man's political beliefs are his own. Surely, you don't deny that!

ACCOUNTANT: Even if he was a Communist!

ARCHIBALD: *tired*   When all else fails, call him a Communist.

MATRON: Spent the last month in Russia!

ARCHIBALD: Feeble, Matron. Bethune and his wife may have gone to Russia, but so did a couple of hundred other doctors and their wives from this continent to the World Physiological Conference in Moscow. Anyway, Bethune and the other two doctors from Montréal who went are speaking at McGill tonight, so go along and judge for yourselves. Now, if there isn't anything more convincing than you've put forward, I think we can drop the whole subject of cashiering Bethune.

MATRON: *wailing*   It's not fair. He's so rude. He comes into the hospital dressed in turtleneck sweaters.   *She sobs.*   When I said something to him about it . . . . *Sobbing again.*   . . . he came in the next day as a lumberjack! . . . It's awful.

She sobs quietly.

ACCOUNTANT: *comforting her*   Now, now, dear.

DIRECTOR: Doctor, this man has done nothing but disrupt this unit since he's been here.

ARCHIBALD: Done nothing! Only published ten scientific papers, all of them concise, timely and based on sound inventive research. He's researched, developed and designed a score of ingenious surgical instruments now manufactured and used internationally. Done nothing! He's achieved more in three years than most surgeons achieve in a lifetime. All of which has promoted the prestige and reputation of this hospital.

DIRECTOR: Perhaps. But he's destroyed the unity and
    "l'esprit de corps" of the staff. He's turned many of
    the surgeons who work in the clinic *against you*!

ARCHIBALD: How?

DIRECTOR: He says you take perfection to a ridiculous
    extreme.

ACCOUNTANT: That you operate too slowly.

MATRON: He says that you're such a perfectionist that
    once, when you were operating, the nurse told you the
    patient was dead, and you said . . .   *Beat.*   I know,
    but I haven't finished the operation.

ARCHIBALD: Nonsense! That story was being told about
    me long before Bethune got here. Bethune thinks I
    operate too slowly. He feels I endanger my patients' lives
    by keeping them under the anesthetic too long. That
    they'll die of post-operative shock. I feel he operates too
    fast, thereby running the risk of his patients dying of
    post-operative hemorrhage. Who's right? The whole
    surgical world is about equally divided on the subject.
    Until we improve our anesthetics, no one is absolutely
    right! So don't accuse him of turning my staff against
    my surgical methods. They were divided long before he
    came!   *Beat.*   Now, that's enough! I don't want
    anymore of these "witch hunts" unless there is just
    cause! I suggest you get back and do some real soul
    searching! Good morning!

The Trio rises as ARCHIBALD exits.

DIRECTOR: *to ARCHIBALD*   Mark my words. This
    man has all the full-blown instincts of a lemming. He'll
    throw himself over the cliff. Nobody will have to do it
    for him. You wait and see. Just wait. Let's just hope he
    doesn't drag us over with him.

After ARCHIBALD's exit, the Trio reseat themselves in unison as they become audience for BETHUNE's speech. BETHUNE enters with FRANCES. She sits upstage. BETHUNE arranges his notes for the following public speech. There is a spotlight on him.

BETHUNE: You have heard my colleagues' impressions of the Soviet Union, and I am sure they all satisfied you with their funny stories of the absurd hotels and the ludicrous tourist services. Possibly confirmed all the prejudices you already had, before you came here, on that country.   *Pause.*   I too saw many things that annoyed and amused me. Like the boast that there were no prostitutes in Moscow. Rubbish! However, I did have some positive responses to the trip . . . I appeared to be the only traveller who was deeply impressed with their system of hospitalization, welfare and social medicine. However, our varying opinions of the USSR point up the only real conclusion that does emerge. Whatever anyone says about Russia is relatively true. Not in any absolute terms, of course.   *Pause.*   Soviet Russia is an enigma, a paradox. What I saw reminded me of something Isadora Duncan wrote in the story of her life. She describes how she, or any other woman, must look in the act of giving birth. "There I lay," she wrote, "a fountain of spouting blood, milk and tears." What would a person think watching for the first time a woman in labour and not knowing what was occurring to her? Would he not be appalled at the blood, the agony, the apparent cruelty of the attendants, the whole revolting technique of delivery? He would cry, "Stop this, do something, help, police, murder!" Then tell him that what he was seeing was a new life being brought into the world, that the pain would pass, that the agony and the ugliness were necessary and always would be necessary to birth. Knowing this, then, what could he say truthfully about this woman as she lies there? Is she not ugly? Yes. Is she not beautiful? Yes. Is she not pitiful, ludicrous, grotesque and absurd? Yes. Is she not magnificent and sublime? Yes. And all these things would be true.   *Beat.* Now Russia is going through her rebirth and the midwives and the obstetricians have been so busy keeping the precious baby alive that they have not got around as yet to cleaning up the mess. And it is this mess, the ugly, uncomfortable and sometimes stupid mess which affronts the eyes and elevates the noses of those timid male and female virgins suffering from frigid sterility of the soul, who lack the imagination to see behind the blood the significance of birth. Creation is not and never has been a genteel gesture. It is rude, violent and revolutionary! But to those courageous hearts who believe in the unlimited future of man, his divine destiny which lies in his own hands to make of it what he will, Russia presents today the most exciting spectacle of the evolutionary emergent and heroic spirit of man which has appeared on this earth since the Renaissance. To deny this is to deny your faith in man and that is the unforgivable sin, the final apostacy.

The lights go up and the Trio clap unenthusiastically.

ACCOUNTANT: *sarcastically* Well, wasn't that elevating?

DIRECTOR: Yes. Wasn't it. *Beat. His* final apostacy!

ACCOUNTANT: Red as a raspberry.

MATRON: What can we do?

DIRECTOR: Nothing.

ACCOUNTANT: Nothing!

DIRECTOR: Nothing. Can't you see he's putting his head in the noose all by himself. An outcast, socially. Now, politically. The next thing he'll do is destroy himself medically. Just wait. A lemming.

MATRON: What about Archibald?

DIRECTOR: *impatient* Wait. Just wait. Even Archibald won't be able to defend him.

62

ACCOUNTANT: My God. I don't believe it.

MATRON: What?

ACCOUNTANT: Do you see what I see? Look!

DIRECTOR: Dear God. Louis Kon.

ACCOUNTANT: A card carrying Communist. Oh, this is precious.

MATRON: Delicious.

DIRECTOR: Come on.

They all rise and tiptoe off in unison.

KON: Doctor. Enjoyed your speech very much. It took considerable courage.

BETHUNE: Hmm. Courage, did it? You're Louis Kon, aren't you?

KON: Yes.

BETHUNE: Mr. Kon, please don't misunderstand. What I saw in Russia did not convert me to Communism.

KON: But your admiration for the Revolution . . .

BETHUNE: For the *Russian* Revolution. Yes. This is not Russia. What the Russians did through revolution, we can do through reform. This country has had centuries of democratic tradition. Russia had none. Here, reform will work.

KON: And if *reform* fails?

BETHUNE: It won't. My God, man. Do you think that people are fools? Many citizens and doctors alike realize the present practice of medicine is determined by Capitalism, a system facing a serious economic crisis.

You and I will see an equitable system of socialized medicine and soon. Because the people will demand it. Through *reform*, not revolution.

KON: I wish you every success with your plan for medical reform, but I think you are naive.

BETHUNE: Naive?

KON: Naive. I don't believe that the medical profession will take your plan seriously, in spite of the grudging esteem they have for you. Because the rest of the Committee who drafted this plan are laymen. Primarily writers, painters, artists.

BETHUNE: Who better than artists?   *Beat.*   The function of the artist is to disturb, to arouse the sleeper and shake the complacent pillars of the world. In a world terrified of change, it is the artist who preaches change, the principle of life. It had to be the artists. You didn't expect the doddering gargoyles of the C.M.A. or the A.M.A. to preach reform, did you? And the medical profession will accept it because they are too unimaginative to put up any logical defence to something which is so evidently right.

KON shakes his head.

BETHUNE: You shake your head.

KON: Because, my dear fellow, you are naive. Beautifully naive. But naive nevertheless. I recently read that you said "the initial lure into the practice of medicine for many of your colleagues was the fact that it could be 'the golden egg,' the springboard to the upper levels of society, self-esteem and wealth."

BETHUNE: Correct, but . . .

KON: Consequently for such men, money and social distinction is the primary motivation.   *Beat.*   With equity and the relief of human suffering of secondary importance. And it is these men who will destroy you. You will find that people will give up their sons in war, even their own lives. They will even give up their freedom as they have in Germany and Italy, but they will never give up their money. They will only yield when a stronger power and force than they can *buy* takes over, and then only after a great struggle, and that struggle is called Revolution.

BETHUNE: I am not convinced. And certainly not ready to throw my lot in with you and you can see why! Even talking to you has completely emptied this hall. Good evening, Mr. Kon.

KON: Doctor, before you go, I would like to give you this. "Moscow Dialogues."

BETHUNE: *taking the book and glancing at the table of contents* I'll read the book. Thank you. Come on, Frances.

Scene 6

COLEMAN is preparing a tray of drinks. The doorbell rings. It rings again. COLEMAN goes to the door.

COLEMAN: *to BETHUNE*   You great clod. Why are you ringing the doorbell? You've got a key.

FRANCES: Don't talk to him, R.E. He is in one of his black moods. He rang the doorbell to annoy *me*.

BETHUNE: Well, you keep reminding me it's not our home.

FRANCES: Ignore him, R.E. He's mad because I suggested that little man . . .

BETHUNE: Mr. Kon.

FRANCES: Mr. Kon should be locked up. I wasn't being serious. Really.

COLEMAN: *jovial*   And so he should be locked up, dear. And so should you.   *To BETHUNE.*   You vicious brute. Upsetting all those people tonight.

BETHUNE: So you made it. I didn't see you.

COLEMAN: Hiding at the back of the hall. Don't want to be seen at these left-wing gatherings.

He winks at FRANCES.

BETHUNE: Oh, alright you two.   *He goes to the tray of drinks.*   Booze!

COLEMAN: All poured, your majesty. Here's yours, love. Nice and dry.

FRANCES: Thank you.

COLEMAN: *holding up his glass to FRANCES*
"Give him strong drink
Until he wink
That's sinking in despair;
An' liquid guid to fire his bluid,
That's prest w' grief and care;"

He falters.

FRANCES:
"There let him bowse and deep carouse,
W' bumpers flowing o'er,
Till he forgets his loves or debts"

BETHUNE: "An' minds his griefs no more."

COLEMAN: Aha!

He drinks.

BETHUNE: Who's been teaching you Robbie Burns?

COLEMAN: Frances. Who else? You don't know what we get up to while you're off cavorting with the Socialist hordes.   *He picks up the Scotch and pours some into BETHUNE's glass.*   Top the man up.   *Pause.* Oh, come on, Beth. What's up?

BETHUNE: Sorry, R.E. You too, love. It's me. I'll be alright in a minute. Still pissed off about tonight.

FRANCES: I can't imagine why.

COLEMAN: Perfectly rousing speech. I was almost ready to rush out and burn down the Houses of Parliament. *Laughing.*   Only my foot was asleep.

BEHTUNE: *laughing*   Bastard.

COLEMAN: Seriously. It wasn't bad.   *Beat.*   Course, it's a load of cods-wallop!

BETHUNE: What do you mean?

COLEMAN: The marvels of the Revolution.

BETHUNE: In the eighteen years since their Revolution, the Russians cut down the incidence of tuberculosis by fifty percent.   *Beat.*   By simply instituting free medical care. That's cods-wallop.

COLEMAN: Cut it down fifty percent! Stalin has simply knocked off fifty percent of the population with his purges.

BETHUNE: He's knocked off no more people than the Yankees did after their Revolution.   *Beat.*   Ask the Empire Loyalists!   *Beat.*   And not nearly as many as the French did after theirs.   *He mimes a guillotine with his hands.*   And look at the people we're knocking off everyday.

FRANCES: *What* are you talking about?

BETHUNE: When I say we, I mean the medical profession.

COLEMAN: You're not exactly deliberately murdering them though. Like Stalin.

BETHUNE: Aren't we? I could have pointed out at least a dozen surgeons in the audience tonight who personally murder patients regularly! Refill.

COLEMAN pours him a refill.

BETHUNE: I include myself.

COLEMAN: Personally murder!

FRANCES: Beth. This is going a bit far.   *Lightly.* Oh, come on.

BETHUNE: I'm serious.

There is a beat.

COLEMAN: *interested*   Go on.

BETHUNE: Case in point. Ward B.

COLEMAN: Ward B.

BETHUNE: Ward B. Your equivalent of Death Row. I think there are about twenty there now. We murdered a couple today.   *Beat.*   Everyone on Ward B is going to die. Not because they're incurable, but because no one will operate on them.

COLEMAN: They're not incurable, but no one will cure them. I don't believe you.

BETHUNE: Don't then.

FRANCES: Oh, Beth.

COLEMAN: You don't mean to tell us that no one will operate on them because they're penniless or something.

BETHUNE: No. Not because they're penniless. Although most of them are. Who isn't these days? No, some of the victims on Ward B are quite wealthy actually.

COLEMAN: I'll bite. Why *not* operate then?

FRANCES: Yes. This is getting a bit bizarre. Is this some kind of joke?

BETHUNE: No. *Beat.*   You see the people on Ward B all have severely advanced tuberculosis. Their only chance of survival is surgery. But no one will operate because they are bad surgical risks. They have about a ten percent chance of making it through the operation alive.

COLEMAN: And if they make it through, would they be okay?

BETHUNE: Certainly.

COLEMAN: And do these people want to be operated on?

BETHUNE: Without exception.

FRANCES: Even though they know they have only a slim chance of surviving the operation?

BETHUNE: They know the odds.

COLEMAN: Then why not operate?

BETHUNE: You agree then, that not to do so is surely a mild form of murder!

COLEMAN: Perhaps. *Beat.*   You still haven't explained why you don't operate.

BETHUNE: It's all to do with batting averages. You see, while the practice of medicine is like professional baseball, there will always be Ward B's. A pro baseball player is paid on the basis of his reputation. His batting average! Would you go to a surgeon who had the reputation of losing large numbers of patients on the operating table? Of course not! And while our pocket books are tied to our reputations, we will continue to slink past Ward B.

COLEMAN: Not exactly murders.

BETHUNE: I don't know. Sins of omission. Maybe the whole world is turning into a Ward B.

COLEMAN: Oh?

BETHUNE: Have you read that little madman in Germany's book?

FRANCES: "Mein Kampf."

BETHUNE: In "Mein Kampf," he says he will exterminate all the Jews!

COLEMAN: You don't believe that!

BETHUNE: A lot of people do. Anyway, I'm putting forth a hypothetical question. If he started slaughtering the Jews as he promises and we closed our eyes, slinking past Ward B, so to speak, wouldn't we be silent co-conspirators in their liquidation?

COLEMAN: I suppose.

BETHUNE: And now you see what pissed me off tonight. I'm not trying to be a harbinger of gloom. Maybe Hitler won't murder the Jews. But believe me, Fascism is a deadly disease. And its spreading too fast.   *Beat.* Not spreading because there are millions of Fascist fanatics in the world, but because we let the disease spread by not giving a damn. Fascism, to the average German, is having an ice-box full of sauerkraut. Mussolini, to the average Italian, is having the trains run on time. For the first time in their history. The average Joe Blow doesn't bother looking into what these madmen are really doing. And when someone like Louis Kon tries to tell us, we wish we were somewhere else. Clear the halls!

FRANCES: Louis Kon didn't mention Fascism.

BETHUNE: He said, "People will give up their sons in war, even their own lives, even their freedom as they have in Germany and Italy, but they won't give up their money." He might just as easily have said their ice-boxes of sauerkraut or their train schedules. He was talking about Fascism.

FRANCES: You disagreed with Louis Kon. Now you agree with him. Honestly, you argue for the sake of argument.

COLEMAN: Surely you don't believe the Fascists will take over here!

BETHUNE: There was a Fascist rally here just last night — right here in Montreal.

COLEMAN: Yes. But they're a joke. No one takes them seriously.

BETHUNE: Hitler was a joke in Germany at one point.

COLEMAN: There's more chance of the Reds taking over than the Fascists.

BETHUNE: Exactly the sentiment that allowed Hitler and Mussolini to rise to power.

COLEMAN: Oh, come on. *Beat.*   This is getting a bit heavy. This was supposed to be a little celebration. I've missed you both since you've been away. Especially you, dear. I've been practising up my Robbie Burns. Want another rendition?

BETHUNE: Spare us. *Beat.* But not the Scotch.

He drains the bottle.

FRANCES: Beth, are you trying to get drunk? Honestly, sometimes you're a pill.

COLEMAN: Isn't he though. *He goes to the empty bottle.* We're dry.

BETHUNE: I'm getting anesthetized. Besides, they don't have Scotch in Russia. Just vodka. And I can't stand vodka.

COLEMAN: Let's dance. *He picks up a record. To FRANCES.* I'll get the phonograph.

BETHUNE: No. I'll provide the music.

He goes and winds up the Wee Willie Winkie music box.

FRANCES: Beth!

BETHUNE: No, you make a lovely couple. *He pushes them together, roughly. To COLEMAN.* You're perfect because you own the French Impressionists and . . . *To FRANCES.* . . . you're perfect because you match them so perfectly. *Beat.* You deserve each other.

He goes to the door.

FRANCES: Where are you going?

BETHUNE: To march in the May Day Parade. *Beat.* No, to get more Scotch. *He digs into his pocket.* I think! *He pulls out a $5.00 bill.* Ah! *He examines the bank note.*

BETHUNE:
"Wae worth thy power, thou cursed leaf!
Fell source o' a' my owe and grief,
To FRANCES.   For lack o' thee I lost my lass,
And for lack o' thee I scrimp my glass!"

FRANCES: Ha! Let me answer with another wee drop
o' Robbie Burns!   *Beat.*

"While Europe's eye is fix'd on mighty things,
The fate of empires and the fall of kings;
While quacks of State must each produce his plan,
And even children lisp the Rights of Man;
Amid this mighty fuss just let me mention,
The Rights of Woman merit some attention."

BETHUNE: Hmmm.   *Beat.*   Well, *have fun.*
To COLEMAN.   You'll have your work cut out for
you.

COLEMAN: God, what's got into him?

FRANCES: Oh, come on. Let's dance.

They waltz. The lights fade to black.

Scene 7

*The Trio and ARCHIBALD enter as in the previous "Trio
scene."*

ARCHIBALD: This better be more important than my
coffee break.

*The MATRON and the ACCOUNTANT nod at the
DIRECTOR, who stands up.*

DIRECTOR: *handing a folder to ARCHIBALD*   Weekly
surgical report. I draw your attention to page three.
Dr. Bethune's surgical record as of the last six days.

*ARCHIBALD puts on his glasses and reads. He slowly stands,
incredulous.*

ARCHIBALD: *unsure* Surely there's some mistake . . .

He looks at the Trio, then sits down.

DIRECTOR: You realize as director I must demand his
instant dismissal. I understand your personal feelings.
Beat. We'll make every effort to hush it up.

MATRON: For the good of the clinic.

ACCOUNTANT: Your reputation.

DIRECTOR: There is a position open in a French-
Canadian institution outside of Montreal. We could
make it look as if he wanted to branch out on his own.

MATRON: A Catholic hospital. Sacré-Coeur.

ACCOUNTANT: We've made the arrangements.

MATRON: He'll be happier there with the nuns.

DIRECTOR: It's for his reputation as well as ours. It's
for the best.

ARCHIBALD: *emotional* Where is he?

DIRECTOR: Be here shortly.

MATRON: We thought you would probably want to
tell him yourself.

ACCOUNTANT: *righteous* He's a butcher!

MATRON: Treated them like guinea pigs. Butcher!

*The DIRECTOR hushes them with a gesture. He realizes
the awful impact the report has had on ARCHIBALD.*

DIRECTOR: It's a bitter blow for you, isn't it?   *Beat.*
I warned you he was a lemming! I'm sorry.

ARCHIBALD: Please.

*He motions for them to leave. They exit in unison, a little
less militant. BETHUNE enters. He is silent. They stare
at each other.*

ARCHIBALD: Why?

BETHUNE: Why did sixteen patients out of twenty die
under my knife in the last week? Eighty percent
mortality rate for the tabloids.   *Beat.*   A twenty
percent "success rate." For Ward B. Depends on how
you look at it.

ARCHIBALD: *angry*   Beth! God damn you! I asked
why! I know you cleaned out Ward B. Lord knows,
I've crept past it often enough myself. I asked you
why! The real WHY! Why did you commit professional
suicide? You know you're finished here, even if we do
hush it up. *But why?* Your years of brilliant work!
Beat.   Your reputation, your ideals, your hopes of
reform down there in the morgue.   *Beat.*   *Why!*

BETHUNE: Perhaps it's because I'm sick of going to
meetings of the American Association of Thoracic Surgery
and hearing papers by the biggest names in the business
telling us of their remarkable achievements in thoracoplasty
operations with their *amazingly* low mortality figures.
Beat.   *How* we praise and admire them and their
statistics! Even if we all know they've got their amazing
surgical records by *choosing* only favourable cases.
Refusing operations . . .

ARCHIBALD: *interrupting him*   Rubbish! It won't
wash! You already blasted out that opinion at the last
meeting of the Association in Boston. You didn't have
to demonstrate it here.   *Pause.*   Now, *why?*
Beat.   God, I have a right to know. I engaged you,
defended you, even admired you.   *Beat.*   Dear God,

you've caused me enough trouble. Your rows with the staff. Your unpardonable rudeness, your eternal questioning of everything. Your embarrassing political manoeuvres. Now this! *Why!* *A pause, then, something begins to dawn on ARCHIBALD.* You don't know why, do you? *Pause.* You have a vision of truth, keen and narrow, as if you wear blinkers, but you don't know what that vision is! You tread on toes without knowing it and even if you did know, you wouldn't care. You think all of us are mercenary, in spite of the fact that a great many of us are as concerned and dissatisfied with the present form of medical practice as you are. *Pause.* Well, I'm glad you're leaving. *Beat.* A ship without a pilot is a hazard to navigation *and that's you!* *Beat.* I always saw those three musketeers who constantly parade in here as three frightened mice, three minor officials terrified of change, but they had more insight than I had. They were right. YOU'RE A DANGEROUS MAN!

BETHUNE: The trouble is that, by nature, you shoot butterflies with a shotgun and I hunt elephants with a bow and arrow.

ARCHIBALD: What are you talking about!

BETHUNE: You stand in your twelve by twelve cocoon of an operating room surrounded by efficient "linen crisp" attendants meticulously operating on *someone's toenail*! While outside, there's a vicious virus germinating and spreading that will throw us back into a new dark age and fill a casualty ward that will stretch from horizon to horizon. *He pauses as he goes to the door.* It's like a bad dream. *Beat.* I had to do something. But what? *Beat.* I started on Ward B.

The lights fade to black.

Scene 8

COLEMAN enters. He is dressed in his pyjamas and a rather smart dressing gown. He carries a cup of cocoa. The doorbell rings.

COLEMAN: *opening the door* Frances!

FRANCES: I'm sorry, R.E., Beth has the keys. Did I wake you?

COLEMAN: No. *Beat.* What's wrong? Where's Beth?

FRANCES: Out there somewhere.

She is on the verge of tears, but she calms down.

COLEMAN: Want some cocoa?

FRANCES: *shaking her head, pausing* I can't take anymore. I can't!

COLEMAN: Come on, sit down. What happened? Did you go to the Rutherfords?

FRANCES: *nodding* God knows why they invited us. Beth's rudeness has become legendary. You know how he can perform at these stuffy dinner parties. Well, tonight was his "coup de théâtre." Why he gets this juvenile delight out of shocking people beats me.

COLEMAN: He didn't piss on the aspidistra?

FRANCES: That was at the Stanley's. No, he was much more subtle this time. He opened with his usual statements about how dull, insensitive and unaware the people in the room were. *She imitates BETHUNE.* "The wealthy cocooned in their wasteful, ignorant little world while Hitler's gassing the insane, Franco's at the gates of Madrid, and there are breadlines at their doors" etc., etc. The usual Bethune "patented" line. Guaranteed to aggravate at least half of your guests before they've finished their first martini. Then, of course, he got into politics. *She pauses and looks worried.* Then he passed around this little card.

COLEMAN: Card?

FRANCES: He's joined the Canadian Communist Party!

COLEMAN: *rising, concerned*   You're sure this wasn't one of his jokes?

FRANCES: No, I don't think so.

COLEMAN: *pacing back and forth*   He's been going to these meetings with Kon, but I didn't think for one minute he'd join them. God, he'd better keep it quiet out at Sacré-Coeur. The nuns pray daily for Francisco Franco. They think he's a knight of the Church, a bulwark against the anti-Christ of Communism.

FRANCES: He said he showed it to the Mother Superior today and she ran away from him as if he was the devil incarnate.

COLEMAN: Oh, God.   *Beat.*   Then he's finished.

FRANCES: So am I.

COLEMAN looks at her. He's heard this before, but he knows now she's somehow serious.

FRANCES: Oh, it's not this Communism business. It's Beth. Sometimes I think he's mad. Or maybe I'm mad. Maybe he's right. The whole world's mad.

COLEMAN: What will you do?

FRANCES: Divorce, I suppose. It will be easier this time.

COLEMAN: Frances.   *Beat.*   Don't be too hasty.

FRANCES: Hasty! God, you've seen what he's been like.

COLEMAN: It's been a difficult time for him. This socialized medicine thing up in smoke. Every major party in the election rejected it. Then the medical profession officially scotched it. He's taken it pretty hard. Now he's floating around in a kind of ether. Beth's one of these people who need mountains to climb and right now he's in limbo. Maybe this Communist stuff is just a passing straw he's grabbing at.

FRANCES throws up her hands in despair.

COLEMAN: God, he must have raised a few eyebrows at the Rutherfords. A card carrying Communist in their midst.

FRANCES: Oh, he wasn't satisfied with that! That was just the curtain raiser. He got into an argument with some "fund raiser" from the Conservative Party about the class struggle and the free enterprise system. Suddenly, he burst out of the room and returned half an hour later with a prostitute on his arm!   *Beat.*   He gallantly filled her plate from the buffet, poured her a drink, then calmly walked her around the room asking all the business types their professional opinion on what her true market value was! I don't know how it ended. I called a cab and left.

COLEMAN: You know, Beth, I admit he's not your average dinner guest, but *you know that.* You married him — twice.

FRANCES: I don't have the stamina for it anymore.

COLEMAN: Are you serious about . . .

FRANCES: Divorce.   *Beat.*   Absolutely!

COLEMAN: *walking away*   Will you go back to Scotland?

FRANCES: I haven't thought about it.   *Beat.*   No, I don't think I could go back to that.

COLEMAN: But you'll be leaving.

FRANCES: Well, I can't very well stay here, can I?

COLEMAN: I'll miss you. I don't know if I could get used to living by myself again.

FRANCES: You'll manage.

COLEMAN: And you?

FRANCES: I don't know.

She begins to break. COLEMAN goes and holds her. She begins to calm down.

COLEMAN: Frances.   *Pause.*   Will you marry me? I know it sounds stupid and, to say the least, a little premature. Will you — or should I say, would you?

FRANCES gently breaks away and walks around the room. She pauses.

FRANCES: *determined*   Yes! Yes, I will.

COLEMAN goes over and embraces her again. BETHUNE enters, quite drunk.

BETHUNE: Please don't let me interrupt. I'm delighted to see you've found some way to amuse yourselves in my absence.   *Beat.*   Talking of absence, I shall now make it complete. Pack my little black bag and go.

COLEMAN: Please, Beth . . .

BETHUNE: R.E. Frances. You're made for each other, a perfect match. My blessing.   *Beat.*   I leave on Wednesday for Spain.   *Beat.*   Madrid.   *Beat.* Madrid will be the tomb of Fascism. Madrid is the centre

of the world. Remember, R.E., I don't give her away!
I only lend her. I trust I'll conquer more in Spain than
you're likely to with Miss Prim.   *To FRANCES.*
Yes, you do belong here with the French Impressionists.
"Daddy" would approve. "The Gatlings jammed, the
Colonel's Dead and England's far away."   *Reeling*
around.   Excuse me. I think I'm going to vomit.

He exits accordingly. FRANCES and COLEMAN stare at
each other. The lights fade to blackout.

ACT THREE

Scene 1

There is darkness. The lights come up. The scene jells giving the impression of an inferno. Sounds of gunfire, explosions, artillery are heard. A COLONEL is pacing up and down. Behind him, some SOLDIERS are tearing up paper and putting it in boxes. There is an air of tenseness and fear to the scene. SORENSON sits with his camera and flash.

COLONEL: Señor, this is ridiculous.

SORENSON: Colonel, I'm risking my neck for this story. Give him five more minutes.

COLONEL: Four hours late already. Probably dead.

An explosion is heard, very near. They all hit the floor.

COLONEL: *in Spanish*   Burn that shredded paper. Get that outside.   *He salutes.*   We're getting out. Move, move.   *To SORENSON.*   Come on . . . We can't wait. I have my orders.

BETHUNE: *entering*   Gentlemen.

SORENSON: Bethune!

COLONEL: Doctor Bethune.

BETHUNE: As advertised.

COLONEL: *to SORENSON* Please!

The COLONEL goes over and shakes BETHUNE's hand. He freezes while SORENSON takes a picture of him.

COLONEL: So much for propaganda. Now, Doctor, let us get out of here.

BETHUNE: What's going on?

COLONEL: We're moving our headquarters. The line at University City will break at any moment. Please, we must go. We've prepared another line. We go there now. *In Spanish.* That's all. Move, move . . .

BETHUNE: I'm not going anywhere.

COLONEL: What!

BETHUNE: I'm staying.

COLONEL: Doctor, I don't have time to explain details. Believe me, the front line is one half kilometer away and it's crumbling.

BETHUNE: I've just been there. It won't fall. Those magnificent bastards are treading blood and breathing sparks, but they'll hold.

COLONEL: This is a military matter. Doctor, we are honoured to have your name associated with our cause. But please get back to the hospital. I'm sure you're needed there.

BETHUNE: Your blasted hospital is fifteen kilometers from here. And they don't need me. You've got more doctors than wounded. At least more doctors than wounded who aren't dead on arrival. Ninety percent die from loss of blood before they get to that never-never land of your hospital.

COLONEL: The hospital and headquarters have been moved behind the new line. *Beat.* The civilian government has moved to Valencia.

BETHUNE: *pointing* So those bastards there have already been written off!

COLONEL: *pointing* Doctor, those are a poorly armed mob of militia men and civilians who are trying to hold back 20,000 crack Fascist infantry. They can't hold! We've prepared a new line.

BETHUNE: I throw my lot in with them.

COLONEL: *throwing up his hands* Our cause attracts Communists, Anarchists, Loyalists, liberals, artists, romantics and madmen.

BETHUNE: Look! Give me sixty seconds and listen.

COLONEL: *looking at his watch* Go.

Shell bursts are heard awfully close. Everyone hits the floor, except BETHUNE, who pours some Scotch into a tin cup.

COLONEL: . . . Fifty seconds.

BETHUNE: Listen.

BETHUNE passes some Scotch to the COLONEL, who gulps it down. SORENSON takes a swig. In the following description, BETHUNE employs various stage props etc. to clearly demonstrate his plan to the audience.

BETHUNE: This is the line at University City. This is your goddamn hospital and this, presumably, is your new line of defense. Okay. So, this is no-man's land.

COLONEL: It soon will be.

BETHUNE: It is now. You're losing as many men from
    here to here from loss of blood as you are in this inferno.

COLONEL: Strategically . . .

BETHUNE: *interrupting him*   Alright, alright. So, I
    and my group claim this no-man's land. You've given it
    up. I want written authority to requisition every school
    bus and bicycle in this area. This building we're in now.
    We'll operate a milk-run of blood to the line from here.

COLONEL: Where do you get the blood for here? Not
    from the hospital. We need it for the next battle here.

He points.

BETHUNE: There's people living in my no-man's land.
    Thousands of them. Your propaganda machine tells them
    hourly what you don't believe yourselves. This won't fail.
    I'll get my blood from them. You're a reporter. Make
    up an appeal for donors in this area. On radio and in the
    newspapers. Tell them they'll get buttons.

COLONEL: Buttons!

BETHUNE: Half the people here . . .   *He points on a
    floor map.*   The ritzy area are Fascist sympathizers.
    They'll be delighted to have a blood donor's badge to
    hide behind, if Franco fails. Now, my requisition and a
    squad of militia men to round up vehicles.   *Beat.*
    Oh, Christ! Gasoline?

COLONEL: *resigned*   There's a cache of gasoline here.
    We haven't had time to move it. You can have it, but it
    must be blown up the moment the line falls.

BETHUNE: Okay. Okay. It won't fall. But if it does —
    Boom! You agree then.

COLONEL: *scribbling on a piece of paper*   There's
    nothing to lose.   *Handing him the paper.*   Requisition.
    Your squad will be here in about twenty minutes — if
    you're still here in twenty minutes.

ORDERLY: *in Spanish*   Ready to move out.

He salutes.

COLONEL: *in Spanish*   Let's go.

ORDERLY: *in Spanish*   What about these?

COLONEL: *in Spanish*   Mad dogs and Englishmen.

The ORDERLY shrugs. The COLONEL salutes.

COLONEL: *in Spanish*   Goodbye.

BETHUNE: *to SORENSON*   Aren't you going?

SORENSON: I'm a newsman. And you're news.

BETHUNE: What did he say?

SORENSON: Something to the effect of mad dogs and
     Englishmen . . .

BETHUNE: God.

The firing stops. There is silence.

SORENSON: Hear the birds.   *The sounds of birds and
     a siren are heard.*   Better get out of here. They're
     about to bomb the hell out of us.

The distant hum of aircraft is heard.

BETHUNE: I've seen their air-raids. There's no escape.
     If we're hit, we'll either be killed or wounded; if we're
     not hit, we won't be killed or wounded. There's no
     place to hide. Might as well stay. One place is as good
     as another. Drink?   *Pause.*   Why are you looking
     at me like that?

SORENSON: You're either a genius, a hero or a madman.

BETHUNE: *pausing and grinning*   I'm alive.

The first bombs begin to fall. The lights fade.

Scene 2

COLEMAN is reading a book. FRANCES is sitting, staring straight ahead. There is silence.

COLEMAN: *quietly*   Frances.   *Beat.*   Turn it on!

FRANCES: It upsets you.   *Pause.*   I know it upsets you.

COLEMAN: *It* doesn't upset me. *You* upset me.

FRANCES: I'm sorry R.E. I can't help it.

COLEMAN: It just bothers me, that's all. I mean, he's gone.   *Pause.*   Or has he?

FRANCES: What do you mean?

COLEMAN: Sometimes it doesn't seem to matter whether he's alive or dead.   *Beat.*   His ghost still lingers here, doesn't it?

There is a pause.

FRANCES: It's just hard, that's all.

COLEMAN: It's gone nine.   *He goes to the radio.* Why this nightly ritual anyway? There are still newspapers, you know.

FRANCES: But you can't believe the newspapers. The right-wing newspapers tell you Madrid has fallen and the left-wing newspapers tell you it hasn't.   *Beat.* Who do you believe? I believe the BBC.

COLEMAN turns up the radio.

BBC ANNOUNCER: An announcement is expected from
Buckingham Palace at noon tomorrow.   *Pause.*
The war in Spain.   *Beat.*   Our correspondent in
Barcelona reports that Generalissimo Franco has pulled
back his troops from the University City sector of Madrid.
Beat.   After weeks of heavy fighting, the withdrawal
of the Fascist infantry from its frontal attack on the city
is seen as an important turning point in the war.   *Beat.*
With the lifting of the siege, Madrid is reported to be in
a state of wild jubilation.   *The radio fades.*   Association
football — Leeds United . . .

Scene 3

*Jubilant SPANIARDS and MEMBERS of BETHUNE's
BLOOD TRANSFUSION UNIT enter. Their arms are linked.
They are singing, "My Eyes Are Dim, I Cannot See."
BETHUNE is guzzling wine from a bag. SORENSON enters
with a rather attractive PROSTITUTE on his arm.*

SORENSON: Gentlemen!   *Beat.*   Gentlemen! Your
attention.   *A pause while the crowd quietens down.*
I come directly to you as an envoy from the Contessa
Dona Maria Isabel Beatriz de Alba y Romero's house of
leisure, located in the basement across the street. In
honour of the occasion, the Countess and her ladies in
waiting . . .   *He gives the PROSTITUTE a peck on the
cheek.*   . . . have kindly offered a free night in their
house of delights to all members of the unit! A free night!

PROSTITUTE: A free night! Jiggedy-jig!

*There are cheers and the PROSTITUE is picked up and
carried away. The COLONEL enters with an ORDERLY.
SORENSON regains possession of the PROSTITUTE and
slowly makes for the door with her while BETHUNE's
attention is taken by the COLONEL's entry.*

BETHUNE: *warmly*   Colonel. Well, chaps, look who
     is back.

He shakes the COLONEL's hand.

COLONEL: Doctor, my congratulations. You — all of
     you have been magnificent.

BETHUNE: Thank you. Please join the festivities.

COLONEL: I'm sorry.   *Beat.*   On duty.

BETHUNE: *seeing SORENSON leaving with the
     PROSTITUTE*   Sorenson! Sneaky bastard. Trying
     to creep off with my little Lili.   *He goes and kisses
     the PROSTITUTE's hand.*   It's my turn with her
     tonight. You had her last time.

SORENSON: Hardly fair. I had to pay for it.

BETHUNE: Tough!

SORENSON: Also, we were rudely interrupted by an
     air-raid, so it doesn't count.

BETHUNE: You should have carried on regardless of the
     air-raid. Honestly, Sorenson, for a writer, you're awfully
     unimaginative. Now, hand her over.

BETHUNE kisses her hand once again.

SORENSON: *in good humour*   Oh, alright. Vicious
     little man.

BETHUNE takes the PROSTITUTE from him.

BETHUNE: Sorry, Colonel. Family quarrel. Can I do
     anything for you before I depart for more balmy climes?

COLONEL: Doctor, I would appreciate a word with you . . .
     He smiles around.   . . . in private, if I may . . .

BETHUNE: Alright, you decadent bastards. *He ushers SORENSON, the PROSTITUTE and the SPANIARDS out.* Remember, Sorenson. Hands off.

They all exit except BETHUNE and the COLONEL, who motions the ORDERLY out.

BETHUNE: Colonel?

COLONEL: A number of important matters I must bring to your attention.

BETHUNE: Can you get to the point? I'm aging by the minute, and I don't want to be late for the orgy.

COLONEL: *clearing his throat* First of all, the press.

BETHUNE: Yes?

COLONEL: Since Franco has lifted the seige on Madrid, hundreds of newsmen from all over the world are pouring into the city. *Beat.* They want to talk to one man — you!

BETHUNE: I'm flattered. Delighted to oblige them.

COLONEL: Thank you. *Beat.* I have been asked by my superiors to brief you.

BETHUNE: Brief me! What do you mean, brief me!

COLONEL: It's a delicate point, Doctor. It has come to the ears of my superiors that you have not felt restrained from openly voicing some rather embarrassing views on the competency of the political military leadership in Madrid. *Beat.* We hoped you would refrain from giving these opinions to the international press.

BETHUNE: Okay. *Beat.* Nevertheless, what I've "voiced" is damned right. You say, "leadership." What leadership! The government is a coalition of such strange bedfellows as Communists, Social Democrats and

Anarchists, who've been so busy watching, haggling and backbiting each other that Franco has been able to grab half of Spain without a fight. As for the Military, it's exactly the same situation. Everybody has their own private armies in Madrid — the Communists, Anarchists, Trade Unionists, International Brigades. Nobody knowing what the other's doing. Countermanding each other's orders. It makes organized blood transfusion a bureaucratic nightmare.

COLONEL: So you believe in the Mando Unico.

BETHUNE: The United Command. You're damned right. Every citizen and foot soldier has been screaming for it ever since the Fascist invasion began.

COLONEL: Then you'll be delighted to know, as of this morning, the United Command is a fact. Of course, some people don't like it.

BETHUNE: I'm sure. Nobody wants to have their little private army submerged in a great big one. I'm delighted. That's wonderful news.

COLONEL: Unfortunately, the United Command has only been implemented in the Madrid sector. With Malaga now under heavy siege, we thought we'd wait. It would only confuse the situation. *Pause.* I'm not surprised the international press is chasing you. *Beat.* You've done a remarkable thing since you've been here. From a handful of men carrying blood one half kilometer in an old station wagon, to a massive staff including six Spanish doctors, operating fifty blood transfusion units on a 1,000 kilometer front. It's been called the single greatest contribution ever made to military medicine. *Slyly.* You've created quite a private army of your own.

BETHUNE: *catching on* Is my briefing over?

COLONEL: Of course. Now to the second thing. It will come as an acceptable proposition in the light of your support of the United Command. Your whole unit is to be absorbed into the Sanadad Militar — the Army Medical Corps. You will be given the rank of Major. The highest rank, I might add, that our army has given to any foreigner. *Pause.* You can pick up your uniform at the hospital. *Pause.* Doctor, you're the kind of man that thrives in chaotic conditions . . .

BETHUNE: *interrupting him* And you thrive as a bureaucrat!

COLONEL: Doctor, but you have just admitted that blood transfusion should be organized.

A GUARD goes to the door and returns with a message for the COLONEL.

BETHUNE: What is it?

COLONEL: Malaga has fallen. The army and thousands of civilians are in full flight on the Malaga road.

BETHUNE: I'll round up the boys. We'll get a car on the road with some blood. Tell the newspaper boys, I'll see them when I get back.

BETHUNE exits. Blackout.

Scene 4

MEMBERS of the PRESS enter, two women and two men. They seat themselves stage left. At stage right, sitting at a table facing the PRESS is the COLONEL and GENERAL CALABRAS. Standing behind the GENERAL is an armed GUARD. All the characters on stage have a press release before them.

COLONEL: *standing* Ladies and gentlemen of the press, you have received press releases from our headquarters on the situation in Malaga. *Motioning to the GENERAL.* General Calabras, the gallant defender of Malaga. *Beat.* Perhaps any questions arising from the press release can be directed to him.

FIRST REPORTER: *(male)* It states in the press release that Franco's army attacked heavily on a broad front and the centre of the Malaga line fell. Can the General elaborate on that?

COLONEL: *in Spanish* Can you elaborate on the fall of the central sector of our line?

GENERAL: *in Spanish* I cannot elaborate. Further details will be available after a full military enquiry.

COLONEL: The general says he cannot elaborate. Further details will be available after a full military enquiry.

SECOND REPORTER: It states in your press release that the retreat from Malaga is being carried out in an orderly manner in spite of rumours to the contrary. Can the General elaborate on the retreat?

COLONEL: *in Spanish* Can you elaborate on how orderly the retreat is?

GENERAL: *in Spanish* The retreat is orderly. I cannot elaborate further because of security reasons.

COLONEL: The retreat is orderly. The General says he cannot elaborate further because of security reasons.

A SECRETARY enters and whispers in the FIRST REPORTER's ear.

THIRD REPORTER: Does the General plan a counter attack?

COLONEL: Obviously the General cannot answer that question for security reasons.

94

FIRST REPORTER: I understand Dr. Bethune has just
    arrived back from the Malaga Road. Can we talk to
    him?

COLONEL: I'm sure Major Bethune is very tired. I'm
    sure he'll issue a press release.

*BETHUNE enters stage right, behind the table. He shows
his I.D. to the GUARD.*

FIRST REPORTER: *interrupting the COLONEL*
    Dr. Bethune. Could you describe the retreat from Malaga?

SECOND REPORTER: Was your blood transfusion unit
    in operation?

THIRD REPORTER: *almost desperate*   Any details?
    Please.

There is a pause.

COLONEL: Please, ladies and gentlemen, Doctor Bethune
    is obviously tired.

FIRST REPORTER: *interrupting him*   Doctor.
    Beat.   On the Malaga Road. What did you see?

BETHUNE: Saw.   *Beat.*   . . . The farther we went, the
    more pitiful the sights became. Thousands of children.
    We counted five thousand under ten years of age. And at
    least one thousand of them barefoot, and many of them
    clad only in a single garment. They were slung over their
    mother's shoulders or clung to her hands. The incessant
    stream of people became so dense we could barely force
    the car through them. Our intention had been to proceed
    to where the army was fighting a rear-guard action and
    give blood transfusions to the wounded. But by this time
    we had passed so many distressed women and children,
    we thought it best to turn back and start transporting the
    worst cases to safety. . . . It was difficult to choose which
    to take. Our car was besieged by a mob of frantic
    mothers and fathers who, with tired outstretched arms,

held up to us their children, their eyes and faces swollen and congested by four days of sun and dust. "Take this one." "See this child." "This one is wounded." Children with bloodstained rags wrapped around their arms and legs, children without shoes, their feet swollen to twice their size, crying helplessly from pain, hunger and fatigue. Two hundred kilometers of misery. Imagine four days and four nights, hiding by day in the hills as the Fascist barbarians pursued them by plane, walking by night packed in a solid stream of men, women, children, mules, donkeys, goats, crying out the names of their separated relatives lost in the mob. How could we choose between taking a child dying of dysentery or a mother silently watching us with great sunken eyes, carrying against her open breast her child born on the road two days ago? She had stopped walking for ten hours only. We first decided to take only children and mothers. Then the separation between father and child, husband and wife became too cruel to bear. We finished by transporting families with the largest number of young children and the solitary children of which there were hundreds without parents. And now comes the final barbarism. . . . On the evening of the twelfth, when the little seaport of Almeria was completely filled with refugees, its population swollen to double its size, when forty thousand exhausted people had reached a haven of what they thought was safety, we were heavily bombed by German and Italian Fascist airplanes. The siren alarm sounded thirty seconds before the first bomb fell. These planes made no effort to hit the government battleship in the harbour or bomb the barracks. They deliberately dropped ten great bombs in the very centre of the town where on the main street were sleeping, huddled together on the pavement so closely that a car could pass only with difficulty, the exhausted refugees. After the planes had passed, I picked up in my arms three dead children from the pavement in front of the Provincial Committee for the Evacuation of Refugees, where they had been standing in a great queue waiting for a capful of preserved milk and a handful of dry bread, the only food some of them had for days. The street was a shambles of the dead and dying, lit only by the orange glare of burning buildings. In the darkness, the moans of the wounded children, shrieks of agonized mothers, the curses of the men rose in a massed cry higher and higher to a pitch of intolerable intensity. One's body felt as heavy as the dead themselves, but empty and hollow, and in one's brain burned a bright flame of hate. There were two soldiers killed.

There is a pause.

FIRST REPORTER: In the light of what Doctor Bethune saw, perhaps General Calabras would like to comment on his army's retreat?

There is a beat.

BETHUNE: *rising*   Calabras! Did you say Calabras? Is it that scruffy little bastard Calabras? He handed Malaga to the Fascists on a plate because he refused to co-operate with the Communists on his left flank. Calabras and a million anarchist bastards like him should be lined up and shot!

By now he has been manhandled outside by the GUARD. GENERAL CALABRAS is screaming in Spanish. The COLONEL is trying to usher out the REPORTERS, while at the same time blocking PHOTOGRAPHERS and reassuring the PRESS that BETHUNE has been under heavy strain. The lights fade on the chaos.

Scene 5

The lights come up on BETHUNE, who is seated alone onstage. An armed GUARD is stationed at the door. KON enters showing his I.D. to the GUARD. BETHUNE turns around.

BETHUNE: *overjoyed*   Kon! Kon! What the hell are you doing here?

KON: I was sent over by the Canadian Committee to report on the unit. I got in right after Franco lifted the siege.

BETHUNE: I suppose you know the bastards have put me under house arrest.

KON: Yes! *Beat.* Get your stuff. We're leaving.

BETHUNE: So they're not going to shoot me.

KON: No. They agreed on a better idea. We leave for Canada tonight.

BETHUNE: Canada!

KON: You can serve the Republic better at home. They have doctors, and your transfusion unit is working very smoothly. What they need is money! You've become a hero in the English-speaking press. *Beat.* You're in a position to appeal for money.

BETHUNE: Please, Kon. *Beat.* I don't want to go back to Canada.

KON: *calmly* The speaking tour has already been set up.

BETHUNE: But . . .

KON: Besides you don't have much choice.

There is a beat.

BETHUNE: Persona non grata. Is that it? *A pause, then slightly angrily . . .* For the first time in years, I felt adrenalin in my veins. *Pause.* I've blotted my copybook, haven't I? *Pause.* Kon?

There is silence. KON is inscrutable. The lights fade.

Scene 6

Spotlight on BETHUNE. KON is behind him.

BETHUNE: Now you have heard what thousands of freedom-loving *individuals* are doing for Spain. Our Transfusion Unit. The International Brigades. Those of you at home with your financial support.   *Beat.* But what about our governments? What's the matter with England, Canada, France, the United States? Are they afraid that by supplying arms to the Loyalist forces in Spain they'll start a World War? Why, the World War has already started. In fact, it's in its third stage. Spain, Ethiopia, now China. It is Fascism versus Democracy! *There is applause, then a beat.*   Ernest Hemingway, a man with no political axe to grind recently said, "We have to lick Fascism sometime — and the easiest, best and cheapest way is to do it in Spain!" Let's do it! *A pause, then he gives a determined, clenched fist salute.*   And let's do it in Spain!

The sound of a wild roar of applause is heard. The chant, "For Spain, for Spain" slowly fades. Lights come up as BETHUNE goes over to COLEMAN and FRANCES who are standing stage right. He kisses FRANCES on the cheek and shakes COLEMAN's hand warmly.

COLEMAN: *sincerely*   Magnificent speech.

BETHUNE: Thank you.   *Beat.*   Thank God, it's the last.

FRANCES: Last?

BETHUNE: I've terminated the speaking tour. I leave on the train tonight for Vancouver where I board the Empress of Asia. I'm going to China.

FRANCES AND COLEMAN: *together*   China!

BETHUNE: It's too difficult to explain. It's just . . . things are washed up for me here. *Laughing.* I'm a reject. They've closed the hospitals to me because I'm a Communist. *Beat.* Not that I want that anyway. *Beat.* And I can't go back to Spain. But in China there's a great struggle going on which I can identify with. *Pause.* R.E., do you mind if I speak to Frances alone for a minute?

COLEMAN: No, of course not. *To FRANCES.* I'll wait for you outside.

FRANCES: Beth.

FRANCES clings to him.

BETHUNE: *gently holding her at arms' length* Frances, don't talk. Listen. Please listen. For some reason — neither one of us knows why — we've clung onto each other for all these years in a relationship that never completely satisfied either of us. Yet that same impossible feeling is still alive, isn't it?

FRANCES is speechless with emotion. There is a pause. BETHUNE gives her a handkerchief.

BETHUNE: Forgive me if you can. I'm truly sorry for the unhappiness I've caused you. I was like a clumsy and furious gardener hacking away at a tree — a living tree, in an attempt to make it conform to a preconceived and fantastic design of his own. I know now you must be taken as you are. Not to be changed. R.E. is a good man. He will do that. If he doesn't, he will destroy both you and himself. *Pause.* Frances, I won't see you again. It sounds like something out of a lousy melodrama, but it's a simple fact. So this is goodbye. *A pause, then they kiss passionately.* I'll walk you out. Try and get a smile back for R.E. I don't want to remember you like this.

FRANCES tries to smile.

BETHUNE: Ah, ha.   *Pause.*   Come on.

The lights fade.

Scene 7

The sound of a loud Chinese gong is heard. The lights come up. The scene is a cave in Wu-T'ai Base Hospital. BETHUNE is despondent. He is throwing pebbles into a jar. He appears tired and distraught. He hears a noise.

BETHUNE: Tung! Tung, is that you?

TUNG enters.

BETHUNE: Is it still raining?

TUNG: No, Pai-Ch'iu-en.   *Pause.*   There is a visitor for you.

BETHUNE: Who?

TUNG: Ma.

BETHUNE: Ma!

MA HALL: *entering*   They all call me Ma. Good evening, young man. Please don't stand. Tung tells me you're a bit down in the mouth.

BETHUNE: Tung did, did he? Who are you?

MA HALL: I've spent forty years of my life in these mountains — I'm a missionary. I've come to examine you.

BETHUNE: Oh?

MA HALL: Humm. *Beat.* I see you have a full-blown case of "China Fever." Excuse me. Back in a jiffy.

She exits.

BETHUNE: Tung, what the hell's going on? *Pause.* Don't give me the inscrutable treatment. This old duck is completely wacky.

MA HALL: *entering with a bottle* They also say she's deaf. Drink this.

BETHUNE: *gulping down some of the drink, holding his throat, then coughing* What in hell is it?

MA HALL: The local rice brandy. Apparently marvellous for picking up one's spirits.

BETHUNE: I've often taken booze as a sedative for depression, but I've never had it prescribed by a missionary before.

MA HALL: Doctor, please sit down. The booze will not cure the special kind of depression you have. We call it "China Fever." Every young missionary and idealist who comes here to do great things gets it. *Beat.* You see, China is so different. And when one meets China, it is very depressing.

There is a pause. BETHUNE holds back, then he boils over.

BETHUNE: *kicking over the jar of pebbles* God! Who wouldn't be depressed? When I came, it was exhilarating. I met Mao Tse Tung. We talked till the early hours of the morning. Everything seemed possible. I had a team then. A nurse, a surgeon, a caravan of medical supplies and full financial support from an outfit called the China Aid Council in New York. Now, I sit. *Beat.* Alone. In what is colourfully called the 8th Route Army Base Hospital, consisting of fifty caves cut in the side of a mountain. Each cave crowded with gangrene, lice-ridden men huddled together in soiled, tattered uniforms, lying on beds of dirty, matted straw. Surrounded by well-meaning peasants who don't know the first thing about nursing care or basic sanitation. As for my team! Ha! The surgeon was recalled to his mission hospital. The nurse has gone back to Sian and most of my medical supplies are gone. As for the China Aid Council, they've folded. God knows why. So I sit here in the mountains — the whole region completely surrounded by the Japanese — trying to give medical attention to 40,000 soldiers. With more instruments in my little black bag than the whole 8th Route Army Medical Corps.

MA HALL: So. *Beat.* Now you have met China. Inscrutable, merciless. When I came here as a girl, I thought I would accomplish wonders. I suppose I believed in "the White Man's burden." But the astronomical proportions of this sea of misery overwhelmed me. Browning summed up exactly how I felt. *Beat.* "I give the fight up. Let there be an end, a privacy, an obscure nook for me. I want to be forgotten, even by God." *Beat.* I wanted to go — get away! *Beat.* But I stayed. Now you must decide. Either accept the impossible magnitude of your task, or go — and go quickly — before it smothers you.

BETHUNE: I have no intention of going. It's just . . . where do I begin?

MA HALL: *Begin* with the people. Use them. You can't even scratch the surface without their help.

BETHUNE: I can't even speak the language.

MA HALL: You have a good interpreter. And you'll be surprised how many of the people here can read and write. It was the first thing the Communists did for the peasants.

BETHUNE: *Beat.* I think I can straighten out a lot of the sanitary problems, but my biggest problems are medical supplies and trained staff.

MA HALL: Well, I can get your medical supplies.

BETHUNE: Where?

MA HALL: From Peiping.

BETHUNE: Peiping! You'll have to go through the Japanese lines.

MA HALL: I have a British passport. I'm a neutral.

BETHUNE: You know as well as I do, if they find out you're helping the partisans, they'll shoot you.

MA HALL: They wouldn't dare! I'll be back in about five weeks. Give me a list of the things you need.

BETHUNE: Alright. In your honour, Ma, I will institute a five week plan to try and get this incredible mess into some perspective.

MA HALL: Aha! That's the spirit. I believe the fever is waning. You won't need this.   *She takes the rice brandy from him.*   I'll leave in the early morning for Peiping. Good evening.   *Beat.*   And God bless you.   *She pauses at the door and kisses him on the forehead.*   Goodnight.

There is silence. BETHUNE paces back and forth, thinking.

BETHUNE: Tung! Tung!

TUNG wakes up. BETHUNE draws some columns on a sheet of paper.

BETHUNE: Go and get the names of all the people who are available to work with us. Name in this column — sex here. Then, occupation or trade here. Look for carpenters and blacksmiths. Put a tick next to those names who can read and write.

TUNG: Everyone's asleep.

BETHUNE: Wake them up. After you come back, take this list I'm typing to Ma — for Peiping.

He begins typing. TUNG exits. The lights fade.

Scene 8

The lights come up.

BETHUNE: Tung. Come on.

TUNG: Pai-Ch'iu-en, you have been awake all night!

BETHUNE: I'm fine. Here, I've sorted out the list you got last night.   *Beat.*   Now, first of all, what we have to do is organize a routine.   *He picks up the list.* Our carpenters. Give them these drawings. Tell them I will inspect their work this afternoon.   *As he passes TUNG each sheet . . .*
A — The design for an operating room.
B — A sterilizer.
C — Leg splints.
D — Arm splints.
E — Dressing trays.
F — Stretcher racks.
There is a pause.
Now, the blacksmiths. We have to build a forge immediately.   *He gives TUNG another drawing.* It's simple. Make it of stone. Then I want them to forge copies of some of my instruments. Also, I want this incinerator built.   *Handing him another drawing.* Tell them I will go over the plans with them at two o'clock. Now the list of names.
— *Group One* here. They're mostly children and old people. They are in charge of fly control and basic sanitation. They must wash out all the caves with boiling water and lye. Then the caves are to be white-washed.

— Now *Group Two* — My future nurses. The wounded must have their uniforms removed and cleaned and boiled in lye and water. I'll supervise that.
— *Group Three* — They are to make soap. It means making potash. Here is the procedure. Translate it! Tell them I will inspect their work tonight.
— *Group Four* will make three stills. I'm sure they know how to make them already, but here is a simple design for one anyway. We need alcohol for sterilization.
— *Group Five* here. They will make tags for all the wounded. Write their names and the number of the cave they're in on them. We'll keep a master list here. Later it will be integrated into a system of case history charts. Are you still with me?

TUNG: I think so.

BETHUNE: We will hold a group meeting every morning at ten o'clock to see how things are progressing. Starting tomorrow, I will give the nursing group lectures in basic sterilization procedures and the treatment of minor wounds. Now I realize we have to use *what's here* to do and make everything. Use those kerosene drums from the dump to make the dressing trays. You'll also find old shell casings that can be melted down to make instruments. They can also be sterilized and used for bedpans. Now, wake me in an hour. Then I must get to work on a little pamphlet to be printed and distributed on the treatment of basic wounds.   *Pause.*   Come on, Tung. You've got a lot of translating and running around to do.

TUNG is bewildered, trying to remember what is what. BETHUNE has fallen into a deep sleep. The lights fade.

Scene 9

GENERAL NIEH and BETHUNE enter. TUNG stands at the door.

GENERAL NIEH: In five weeks! Incredible. You have brought us a great deal of enlightenment.

BETHUNE: And you and your people have brought me a great deal of enlightenment. Their Communism is simple and profound. They're not cogs in a regime like Russia, or neurotic or suspicious like they were in Spain, but steadfast and patient with unshakable optimism. I'm training fifty nurses and eighteen peasant doctors. I'm a little unhappy about their lack of medical knowledge, but they study diligently, try to improve themselves and they listen to criticism.

GENERAL NIEH: They greatly admire you. You are a very different kind of foreigner. Not like the missionaries.

BETHUNE: You forget. Ma is a missionary. And on Wednesday, she delivered enough medicine to last us for three months.

GENERAL NIEH: Eh. Ah! But Ma — is Ma. She is a great lady.   *Pause.*   My congratulations on your fine work. Now, I must get back to my headquarters.

BETHUNE: What?

GENERAL NIEH: I must go.

BETHUNE: Like hell. Listen, we've patted each other on the back, bowed in each other's direction several times, now let's get down to business. I didn't ask you up here to exchange niceties.

GENERAL NIEH: *taken back*   Doctor!

BETHUNE: *pausing* General. *Beat.* Please listen. This hospital might look fine to you, but it's useless, obsolete. This blasted hospital is so far from the front we might as well turn it into an old people's home! We're losing ninety percent of the wounded on the thirty-five mile trip over these mountains. I plan to build a Model Hospital here . . . *Pointing to a map.* . . . in this abandoned Buddhist temple at Sung-Yen K'ou.

GENERAL NIEH: That's only three miles from the line!

BETHUNE: Right. It will also double as a training hospital. We might as well forget about getting trained medical help from the outside. I've been working on a complete medical text with over two hundred drawings in it which will train nurses in six months, doctors in eighteen months and surgeons in two years. Between lectures, the students will go from the Model Hospital to the front where they will treat the wounded first hand. Once I have some trained doctors, they'll work in mobile operating units. We've already designed the equipment for these mobile units. It consists of a collapsible operating table and enough instruments and dressings for five hundred operations. All this can be carried on three mules. The operating room can be completely set up and functioning in thirty minutes. This means we can operate right up and down the line no matter how far it may extend.

GENERAL NIEH: But, Doctor, this Model Hospital is too close to the line. This is guerrilla warfare. Combat lines can change overnight. Now your idea of mobile operating units is ideally suited to guerrilla warfare. But our training hospital! It could be overrun by the Japanese at any time.

BETHUNE: We have to risk it. We need trained personnel and the fastest way to teach my students is under actual combat conditions. Hell, it's worth a try. We can have the temple ready in two months.

GENERAL NIEH shakes his head.

108

BETHUNE: Think of the long term advantages. We can keep turning out doctors and nurses for years. Not just to serve the army but the twenty million peasants who live in these mountains. Come on, General. You wouldn't refuse a man on his birthday!

GENERAL NIEH: It's your birthday?

BETHUNE: Celebrated my forty-eighth in Madrid last year — now my forty-ninth in China.

GENERAL NIEH: *pausing* Your birthday. *Laughing.* Suppose I can't refuse.

BETHUNE: Thank you.

GENERAL NIEH: Now I must go. *Gravely.* Happy Birthday.

He exits.

TUNG: Pai-Ch'iu-en, it is not your birthday.

BETHUNE: I know. But I feel like it is.

The lights fade.

Scene 10

BETHUNE is packing his instruments, counting containers, etc. He is about to put on his winter coat when there is a knock at the door.

BETHUNE: Yes!

MA HALL: *entering* Hello, young man.

BETHUNE: *hugging her* Ma!

MA HALL: I've just taken a private tour of your Model
    Hospital. It's most impressive. And all your little students
    studying diligently. I'm sorry I missed the grand opening.

BETHUNE: Well, you're only a week late. How did you
    make out this trip?

MA HALL: I'm afraid the prices have doubled for
    anesthetics on the black market. The Japanese are keeping
    a close watch on everything. But we did what we could.

BETHUNE: Thanks.   *Pause.*   You know, Ma, you
    can't keep making these trips. They're too hard on you.
    They'll catch up to you one of these days.

MA HALL: Don't worry about me.   *Beat.*   Where are
    you going?

BETHUNE: I'm taking out our experimental mobile unit
    for a couple of weeks. General Nieh's launching a small
    scale offensive in the northeast section of our line. We
    want the mobile unit set up beforehand.

MA HALL: You've only had your school open a week
    and you're leaving. What about your students?

BETHUNE: I've given them enough to keep them busy
    for a month. They have the text. I told them there will
    be exams when I get back.

MA HALL: The northeast sector is over one hundred
    miles away.

BETHUNE: It will give me a chance to ride my beautiful
    white mare. She was captured from the Japanese.
    Laughing.   General Nieh gave it to me for a birthday
    present.

MA HALL: Talking of birthdays, young man, have you
    looked in the mirror lately?

BETHUNE: What are you talking about?

MA HALL: How long have you been in China?

BETHUNE: About eighteen months.

MA HALL: Look in the mirror. You've aged twenty years. Operating thirty hours at a stretch, giving lectures, running off to battles. You're going to kill yourself.

BETHUNE: Come on, Ma. Don't mother me.

MA HALL: Now, you listen. You have to slow down. Even General Nieh wants you to take a rest.

BETHUNE: Ma, I've never felt better in my life. I miss a cold beer occasionally and I wouldn't mind going to the pictures or eating a steak sometimes. *Beat.* It's true my teeth need attention. I need new glasses and I've gone completely deaf in one ear, but apart from that, I'm in pretty good shape. And *if* I've aged twenty years at least, I'm a spry sixty-nine. Who knows, Ma, if I keep aging like this, you're going to start looking pretty bloody attractive.

MA HALL: *laughing* Oh, honestly!

BETHUNE: Now, my old dear, I've got to get moving. *He puts on his coat.* Looks like snow. Come on. Show me all the goodies you brought me from Peiping. Then maybe we'll have time for a nice hot cup of *English* tea. We captured a whole case from the Japs. *Pause.* Ooh! Look at her face light up.

He gives her a peck on the cheek. They exit. The lights fade.

Scene 11

VOICE-OVER FOR OPERATION SCENE: Smell of
chloroform and blood. Three o'clock in the morning,
winter, North China, near Lin Chu, with the 8th Route
Army. Why?   *Beat.*   Men with wounds.   *Beat.*
Bandages glued to the skin with blood.   *Beat.*   This
one. Looks about fourteen. Will he run along the road
beside his mule to another harvest? No, he will never run
again.   *Beat.*   Any more? A Japanese prisoner. Lay
him beside this kid. There are no enemies in this
community of pain. Why, they're alike as brothers.
Is this a professional killer? No, he's an amateur in arms.
Workman's hands.   *Beat.*   Another worker in
uniform.   *Beat.*   A million workmen come from
Japan to mutilate a million workmen in China. Will this
Japanese worker benefit by the mutilation of his Chinese
counterpart? How can he gain? Then in God's name,
who will gain? Who will profit from it?   *Beat.*   Did
the Japanese industrialists tell this workman they only
wanted cheaper raw materials, more markets, more
profit?   *Beat.*   No. They told him this brutal war
was for "the destiny of race," "the glory of the Emperor,"
"the honour of the State." He wouldn't have joined the
army if they told him the truth.   *Pause.*   There can
be no permanent peace in the world while big business
dictates government.   *Beat.*   Only wounds.   *Pause.*
Six in the morning.   *He shivers.*   God, it's cold.

*The scene is the northwest sector of the line at night. The sounds
of machine guns, etc. are heard in the distance. Flashes from
artillery are seen. BETHUNE and his mobile unit are at work.
It is obviously cold. They work under the light of a single
pressure lantern. BETHUNE is completing his operation on
the removal of a SOLDIER's eye. He throws a bloody piece of
gauze in a bucket, then sops a piece of cotton wool in the
eye socket and stitches. An ATTENDANT is holding the
eye socket with some forceps.*

BETHUNE: Fong, do the dressing.

He mimes the action. FONG takes over and quickly tapes the SOLDIER's eye.

BETHUNE: Next!

The first stretcher is removed. Another SOLDIER is brought in by YU and WANG, BETHUNE's other assistants.

BETHUNE: *quickly sizing up the situation*   Amputate.
    Beat.   Blood type . . .   *He reads the SOLDIER's dog-tag.*   Whose turn to be blood bottle?

YU steps forward. We see a direct blood transfusion performed. BETHUNE, meanwhile, is cutting the SOLDIER's trouser leg. FONG is administering the anesthetic. The moans of the SOLDIER gradually subside. BETHUNE ties a tourniquet on the leg. Meanwhile, a NURSE is assembling an amputation saw. TUNG enters, carrying a kerosene safety lantern.

TUNG: Pai-Ch'iu-en.   *Beat.*   Pai-Ch'iu-en.

BETHUNE: Wait, Tung!   *He is now sealing off bleeders.*
    Alright, Wang.   *He motions to WANG.*   You can finish.

WANG takes over.

BETHUNE: No.   *He demonstrates the action.*   That's it. Good!   *He goes over to TUNG.*   Now, Tung. What the hell are you doing here?

TUNG: General Nieh sent me.   *Beat.*   Pai-Ch'iu-en.
    The Japanese advanced yesterday.

He is nearly in tears.

BETHUNE: *gently*   Yes, Tung.

TUNG: They have completely destroyed the Model Hospital.

BETHUNE: *pausing* My students? What about my students?

TUNG: They got away. They've gone back to the old hospital at Wu-T'ai.

BETHUNE: *relieved* Go back to Wu-T'ai. *Beat.* The students are to keep working with the text as if nothing had changed. Get a dispatch to General Nieh. *Beat.* Tell him to meet me at Wu-T'ai on the fifteenth. We'll have to reorganize the whole damn thing. *Beat.* Tell Nieh I'm sorry about the Model Hospital. *Beat.* He was right.

BETHUNE turns to go.

TUNG: *softly* Pai-Ch'iu-en. *Beat.* Pai-Ch'iu-en.

BETHUNE turns around.

TUNG: There's something else. The Japanese. *Beat.* The Japanese have captured Ma. *Beat.* They have burned her mission down.

BETHUNE stares at TUNG for a moment, then turns and goes back to he operating table.

BETHUNE: *softly* Let's get going.

Blackout.

Scene 12

The scene is BETHUNE's cave at Wu-T'ai. GENERAL NIEH and BETHUNE are studying a large map.

GENERAL NIEH: This is the military situation. The Japanese have brought in fifty thousand additional troops. According to our intelligence, they will start a large scale offensive right along the line in about ten days. They know they must take this whole region if they are to reach the Pacific. We must hold — but if they attack in ten days, we won't be able to. Our plan is to try and vacate as many troops as we can from the line — and spearhead a lightning attack on Wednesday, on the north bank of the Tang-ho here. That's where the Japanese headquarters are. If we can break through and kill off their general staff, it could set back their offensive for months. By then they'll be held back by the heavy snows. — And we'll hold.   *Beat.*   It's a very dangerous and perhaps foolish move. We expect heavy casualties. But it's our only chance.

BETHUNE: Alright. We'll split up my unit into three mobile units instead of one, using students. Also, we'll set up four mobile hospitals . . .   *Looking at the map.* . . . here, here, here and here, with a temporary base hospital here in the Buddhist temple at Hua-Ta. My peasant doctors range in age from nineteen to twenty-two and know precious little about academic anatomy — but let's hope they can take a leg off or remove shrapnel without killing the patient — or leaving him with a case of sepsis or gangrene.   *Beat.*   We can't expect master surgeons with only three months training, but they've studied and worked damned hard and if they perform well — we'll model our whole training programme on this kind of system — with new students gradually rotating with the more experienced ones in the mobile units.

GENERAL NIEH: We mount the offensive at first light on the seventeenth then.

BETHUNE: We'll be ready.   *Pause.*   God help us.

The lights fade.

Scene 13

The lights come up on the Tang-Ho front. There is little activity except for occasional sniper fire and artillery in the distance. BETHUNE is on a stretcher, his left hand and forearm are bandaged. TUNG is wiping his brow. A GUARD stands upstage. Two STRETCHER BEARERS and a NURSE are whispering stage right. The NURSE is weeping. GENERAL NIEH enters. A GUARD salutes. TUNG goes to NIEH. They whisper. NIEH goes to BETHUNE.

GENERAL NIEH: *in a hushed tone*   Pai-Ch'iu-en.

BETHUNE: You can speak up. I'm not dead yet.

GENERAL NIEH: We're going to move you to the hospital at Huang-Shih-K'ore.

BETHUNE: No need. There's nothing you can do. *He holds up his bandaged arm.*   Blood poisoning. I cut it when I was operating. Careless.   *Beat.* I've tried soaking the damn thing in formalgamate. It's no good, I'm septic.   *He grimaces.*   It's a rather gloomy subject.   *Beat.*   They tell me the attack was a great success.

GENERAL NIEH: We killed their whole general staff including Marshall Abe. They're in a state of absolute confusion.

BETHUNE: Congratulations.

GENERAL NIEH: Pai-Ch'iu-en. Your students were magnificent. Hundreds of operations. Almost no cases of post-operative infection. We estimate a third of the wounded will be able to return to the line within a month.

BETHUNE: I'm delighted.   *Pause.*   Listen, we need
    250 pounds of quinine and 300 pounds of iron
    compounds each year.   *Beat.*   Never buy medicine
    in Peiping again. It costs twice as much as in Shanghai.

There is a pause.

GENERAL NIEH: *holding back the tears*   We're going
    to move you now.

The STRETCHER BEARERS pick up the stretcher.

GENERAL NIEH: Is there *anything* we can do?

BETHUNE: Nieh.   *Beat.*   Tell my wife I've been very
    happy here. Tell her.

*GENERAL NIEH nods. He cannot speak. BETHUNE is
carefully carried off. All the characters take their caps off
as he passes. They freeze. The lights fade as TUNG steps
forward.*

TUNG:
    I wish to tell you of our Doctor.
    Our Doctor Bethune.
    He died on the night of many stars in the sky.
    He knew. We all knew he would die.
    We wept.   *Beat.*   We carried his body.   *Beat.*
    Frail, it had become.   *Beat.*
    Over many lee, over our mountains.
    Through our villages, the people gathered.
    We said: It is our Doctor, Our Doctor Bethune.
    They wept. The heavens wept.
    We will build him a tomb in the hills.

Blackout.

PRODUCTION NOTES

A translation of the English dialogue in the script that is to be spoken in Spanish:

p. 83   Burn that shredded paper. Get that outside.
         Quemen esto y llieven eso afvera.

p. 83   We're moving out. Move, move.
         Tenemos que cambiar de posicion. Vamos, vamos
             . . . rapido!

p. 84   That's all.
         Eso es todo.

p. 84   Move, move.
         Vamos, vamos.

p. 87   Ready to move out.
         Todo est listo mi coronel.

p. 87   Let's go.
         Entonces, vamos.

p. 87   What about these?
         Que hacemos conellos?

p. 87   Mad dogs and Englishmen.
         Hombres locos estos ingleses.

p. 87   Goodbye.
         Adios y buena suerte.

p. 89   Gentlemen! Gentlemen! . . . The Countess . . .
         Señores, la Contessa Dona Maria Isabel Beatriz de
             Alba y Romero.

p. 94   Can you elaborate on the fall of the central sector
             of our line?
         Puede usted elaborar un poco mas sobre la caida
             del sector central de muestra linea?

p. 94 I cannot elaborate further. Details will be available after a full military inquiry.

No, no puedo decir nada mas. Todos hos detalles seran hoco publicos despues de la inquesta militir.

p. 94 Can you elaborate on how orderly the retreat is?
Puede usted decirnos si la retiradada fue ordenada?

p. 94 The retreat is orderly. I cannot elaborate further for security reasons.
Si, la retirada es ordenada, pero no puedo dicir mas por razones de seguridad.

p. 97 Have this man thrown out of here.
Saguen a este hombre de aqui, rapido.

A NOTE TO THE DIRECTOR

You can choose here the words you want:

Idiot   Idiota
Stupid   Estupico
Son-of-a-bitch   Hijo de perra
Wretch   Desgraciado